THE ETHICS OF

Organized Interests,
Political Power,
and the Common Good

D1626999

THE WOODSTOCK THEOLOGICAL CENTER is a nonprofit research center established by the Society of Jesus.

The mission of the Woodstock Theological Center is to engage in theological and ethical reflection on topics of social, economic, business, ecclesial, and political importance. The Center does research, conducts conferences and seminars, and publishes books and articles.

WOODSTOCK

THEOLOGICAL CENTER

Ethics in Public Policy Program

THE ETHICS OF LOBBYING:

Organized Interests,
Political Power,
and the Common Good

GEORGETOWN UNIVERSITY PRESS WASHINGTON, D.C.

Georgetown University Press, Washington, D.C.
© 2002 by The Woodstock Theological Center. All rights reserved.
Printed in the United States of America

10 9 8 7 6 5 4 3 2 1   2002

This volume is printed on acid-free offset book paper.

Library of Congress Cataloging-in-Publication Data

The ethics of lobbying : organized interests, political power, and the
common good
        p. cm.
"Ethics in public policy program"—
Includes bibliographical references.
ISBN 0-87840-905-X (pbk. : alk. paper)
1. Lobbying—Moral and ethical aspects—United States. I. Woodstock
Theological Center
JK1118 .E85 2002
172' .1—dc21

                                                        2002008991

CONTENTS

FOREWORD:

AN INTRODUCTION TO THE PROJECT

ORIGIN OF THE PROJECT

The Woodstock Theological Center is the sponsor of this project. The center does research, conducts conferences and seminars, and publishes books and articles in support of its mission to engage in theological and ethical reflection on topics of social, economic, and political importance. The center is located in Washington, D.C., with a view to engaging in programs in service to the federal government and the development of national legislation and public policy.

The first such two-year project gathered members of government with experts in political science and social ethics, and it issued a book titled *Personal Values in Public Policy: Conversations on Government Decision-Making* (edited by John C. Haughey, S.J.; Paulist Press, 1979). Subsequently, the center sponsored a major day-long conference, "Welfare Reform, Federalism, and the Common Good," in December 1995. The conference's proceedings were made available to the participants and the wider reading public.

Woodstock launched this project on lobbying in 1998 for three reasons. First, lobbying has grown exponentially during the past twenty years to exercise enormous influence on American politics. It has almost become a new profession in that time, and therefore deserves a new review and evaluation.

Second, lobbying has simultaneously fallen under suspicion and engendered critical resentment in some quarters. Its critics would say it supports "special" (i.e., narrow and well-funded) interests and is oblivious to the general well-being of our democratic life and process.

Third, reputable lobbyists have called, therefore, for a clarification of standards and principles for use within their own ranks and as an explanation to the general public of the goals, objectives, and methods of lobbying to forestall misunderstanding and misjudgment. This clarification would provide the lobbying profession with a normative statement parallel to the codes of conduct and ethical practice of the American Medical Association and the American Bar Association.

METHODOLOGY OF THE PROJECT

During the past fourteen years, Woodstock has developed a signature method-ology, which has been used principally with business executives. Four different two-year projects—with many meetings, interviews, and progressive white papers—each led to the publication of a consensus statement. These publications are *Ethical Considerations in Corporate Takeovers* (1990), *Creating and Maintaining an Ethical Corporate Climate* (1990), *Ethical Considerations in the Business Aspects of Health Care* (1995), and *Ethical Issues in Managed Health Care Organizations* (1999), all published by Georgetown University Press.

This methodology follows a four-step process. The first step is *empirical*. The process originates in and remains close to the actual experience of the practitioners—in this case, lobbyists. They share anecdotes, stories, events, and real-life experience to unearth and discover what actually goes on in the lobbying process. For accuracy and credibility, it is indispensable that guidelines for lobbyists originate in the experiences of lobbyists themselves.

The second step is *reflective*. This step entails guided reflection on the stories or experiences that have been shared, asking a range of questions; for instance: What is happening here? Who is doing what and why? What are the outcomes? The aim is to stand back from the few dozen stories and try to see the forest for the trees. The forest, in this case, is a good explanation of what lobbying is today and how it works. The task here is to understand lobbying and to affirm that understanding accurately and to the best of one's knowledge right now.

The third step involves *evaluative decisions*. On the basis of the understand-ing of lobbying gained in the previous steps, this step involves asking questions like these: What do I think about lobbying? What is good, what is bad, and what is somewhere in between? We have already asked the question, What am I doing as a lobbyist? Now the question is, What is the value [and intrinsic worth] of what I am doing?

The criteria or standards for making these value judgments are lodged in one's own conscience. There are no external moral authorities or abstract "eternal truths" to which one can reliably appeal. The relevant criteria are our feelings of peace or anxiety, clarity or confusion, satisfaction or unease. These examined feelings are the barometer or Geiger counter of the integrity of our behavior. Thus, the aim of this step is as much to heighten consciousness and educate conscience as it is to reach recommendations for a code of conduct. Focus group exchanges are especially helpful for this.

This evaluation is interdisciplinary and interactive. Along with individual interviews, evaluation includes small focus groups and larger plenary meetings with participants from different backgrounds, allegiances, and priorities:

- lobbyists, legislators, lawyers, ethicists, political philosophers, and scientists;
- for-profit and nonprofit lobbyists;
- corporate lobbyists and freelance lobbyists; and
- men and women.

This variety is essential for understanding and evaluating what is going on in lobbying because the relevant "what" is a complex of interactions among people with different viewpoints and value systems. No one actor or group has all the truth. In fact, the truth we seek is not a static permanent result at all. It is a dynamic, ongoing process of reflective interaction that admits of constant development, becoming either better (for some or all involved) or worse.

As the practice of lobbying becomes better understood and evaluated from these various perspectives, the participants also come to understand and evaluate their own perspective more realistically. Ideally, the perspectives of each are broadened and enriched. This is crucial for reaching group consensus on how well lobbying is working in our democratic society and how its performance may be improved.

The fourth step is *action*. The principal action on which group consensus is reached is endorsement, publication, and promotion of the standards and guidelines for lobbyists that the process has generated.

Promotion of the guidelines and the process by which they were reached (experience—reflection—decision—action) is the most important part of the cooperative effort. If the publication remains an unread book on a shelf, the whole project has been practically useless. The decision to promote will, therefore, include creatively deciding on a process of promotion.

ORIGIN OF THE PROCESS

Woodstock is a Jesuit center at a Jesuit institution of learning, Georgetown University. The reflective process just described will be familiar to anyone who has gone to a Jesuit school. Jesuit education is not an information download; it is development of the student in his or her capacity to think, to judge, to deliberate, and to decide how to act. All of these activities are rooted in the basic design of human consciousness. These operations are instinctive in humans. Jesuit education exercises students in the recurrent performance of these operations, so that, on graduation, they have learned to do them very well. They have learned, in other words, how to know what is true and to do what is right. And in particular cases, challenges or opportunities in business or government, for instance, they can design and articulate clearly and persuasively a concrete course of action, which is both intelligent and responsible. Former Jesuit students will also know that this process of reflection is exactly what Saint Ignatius Loyola leads a person through in his *Spiritual Exercises.*

Fortunately, however, this basic methodology is adaptable for use, not just by Jesuit students or religious retreatants, but by any person of goodwill. Woodstock's fourteen years of experience has proven that to be the case.

For this publication, special gratitude is in order for the dedicated and talented team who guided this project. Edward B. Arroyo, S.J., was project coordinator and personally interviewed dozens of lobbyists, legislators, and political scientists. Philip A. Lacovara designed and moderated focus group discussions and also provided the legal context within which the project unfolded. As a political and moral philosopher, Michael H. McCarthy unfailingly reminded us of the larger democratic framework of the great "American experiment" within which all exercises of citizenship, lobbying included, must be set. As project rapporteur, Robert W. Gardner had the challenging task of organizing many discussions into a coherent whole and expressing it in clear and intelligible language. Maria Ferrara has assisted in administering this program in innumerable ways, with great proficiency. We also acknowledge the assistance of Jennifer L. Mondino in preparing chapter 4.

Finally, we thank the organizations that have provided financial support for the publishing and promotion of the outcomes of this project: AARP, and Gerald S.J. Cassidy. Lest objectivity and investigative freedom might seem to be compromised, both Woodstock and these benefactors want to be perfectly clear that the funding was sought and given well after the standards and guidelines of this publication had been decided upon; the funding is solely for the publishing and promotional process.

James L. Connor, S.J.
Director, Woodstock Theological Center
Georgetown University

1 IN THEIR OWN WORDS:

LOBBYISTS REFLECT ON THEIR ETHICAL CHALLENGES

We began this project with the clear intention of listening to lobbyists and to those directly engaged in the lobbying process. We thought of starting with larger gatherings of lobbyists to air their perceptions, but eventually we settled upon a series of interviews with individual lobbyists and legislators, as well as with experienced journalists and congressional staffers who are in regular contact with lobbyists.

We conducted approximately fifty interviews, with promises of anonymity, and with the hope for complete candor on the part of those being interviewed. In these interviews, then in three smaller focus groups, and finally in one plenary session with about fifty participants, we asked respondents how, in their experience, lobbying has changed, how it currently "works," and what ethical challenges they encountered in the practice of their profession. We asked them to reflect on two distinct types of challenges, those that arise in the interactions among clients, lobbyists, policymakers and their staffs, and others of a more institutional nature that relate to the role of lobbying in a democratic society.

After reviewing this material, we were able to identify several recurrent areas of concern. We have grouped quotations reflecting these concerns into two sections. The first covers ethical challenges that arise in the interactions among clients, lobbyists, and policymakers. The second covers the enduring influence of lobbying on American democracy.

We have added headings within each section to demarcate some of the ethical challenges that were identified. Although the organizational categories were chosen by the Woodstock team, the quotations are directly from those who were interviewed. Other than this preliminary organization of what we have heard, we have deliberately refrained from adding commentary or analysis to this chapter of this book. We want the lobbyists themselves to have the first word in describing their ethical challenges, in their own words, on the basis of their own experiences.

Some readers may find these direct quotations difficult to follow without editorial commentary, but we believe they accurately set the stage for later chapters where we develop more fully the ethical reflection we are seeking. We expect that some readers will simply want to skip from these "raw data" of our project to the analyses provided in later chapters. At the conclusion of this three-year process, we developed the Woodstock Principles (see chapter 7) as the centerpiece of the entire effort. In these principles, we deliberately attempted to address the ethical challenges that emerged in the original interviews.

ETHICAL CHALLENGES ARISING IN INTERACTIONS AMONG CLIENTS, LOBBYISTS, AND POLICYMAKERS

MONEY TALKS

"There is no question that's the way the system works . . . those with money are likely to be much better off in advocating many issues than those without it. And you can look at it this way, that almost everyone has more than one lobbyist. Many lobbyists are poor too. But in the real world, those who have more money are able to hire professionals. Lobbying is not like going to court and representing somebody in a criminal trial, even though there are some similarities. It is a whole different experience. If you as an individual have a lot of money, you are entitled to spend it. And yes, that gives you a better chance on some things, even though most issues lobbyists go after are really group benefits to a class and the way to lobby those has to pretty much be through a class. . . . I wish poor people could afford to hire professional lobbyists too. But that's the way our system works. I don't know how you resolve this."

"Until the problem of money is dealt with, it is unrealistic to expect the political process to improve in any other respect."

"Deep pockets speak; the money trumps it all."

"The need to raise money constantly is corrupting and demoralizing."

"That's the way the system works. Those with money are likely to be much better off than those without."

CAMPAIGN FINANCE

"There is no question that ethical lapses occur. Sometimes campaign contributions have a disproportionate impact on members' actions. There's also no question but that a lot of times members will do a lot more for you if you have both given and raised money for them than if you haven't."

"One of the ethical challenges is clearly campaign finance, which is a burden on everybody in government. It is a burden on the members, because campaigns are so terribly expensive and they have to spend so much time raising money. The other consequence of that is that they raise so much money [from so many different donors] that it's hard [for one donor] to be particularly important to them. Clearly the system could be improved to relieve the members of the burden of doing this, which consumes from them so much of their time and I think detracts from their being legislators, and creates an appearance to the public that can be a disconcerting cloud over the process."

"There must be some way of prioritizing which interest groups are able to gain access to legislators at different times. At the moment, the prioritization is driven by money. Money seems to be playing a more and more dominant role in American politics: it is becoming a 'pay-to-play' system."

TRUTH TELLING

"You can't lie; what you've basically got is your word and reputation."

"You also can run into situations where people will lie or misstate. Now that is usually self-correcting. It's not considered cool."

"Lobbyists don't want to misrepresent things, because once they do that, once they say something that isn't true, for whatever purpose, they will never be believed again. That's not to say that they believe in what they're saying because obviously it's like being a lawyer. Sometimes you represent a client, you don't necessarily like what they did but you give them the best representation. But lobbyists, my observation has been, really go out of their way not to give wrong information because once they do, they can't take that back. They're gone. . . . That doesn't mean that they don't tell lies. Of course. They try not to go too far with it because once they do they're lost. Lobbyists think about just how much can you shade the picture without losing your own soul, short of that, losing your credibility with the person you're talking to."

"I always say, 'Always tell the truth.' All you've got is your word and if you're providing information, it better be right. And if you find out anything you've told them isn't right, correct it right away. This has to do with effectiveness as well as ethics. To not call people names, to not characterize people in an unflattering way, to try always to be civil, to listen: this is not ethics, it's human dignity. I really do try to tell people when not all the data's on my side. I figure, first of all, they'll find out anyway. But I want to show them I know the data on both sides. But I'll try to be honest, just try not to entrap people. I think any lobbyist should think like that."

"There are two sources of obligation: the mutual obligation of humans to each other, and the desire to avoid public embarrassment and future loss of profits."

"The lobbyist has an ongoing relationship with the people he or she lobbies. In order to be effective, lobbyists should be asking some questions of the client, such as whether the client company is harming workers, because a lobbyist never wants to get into a position where he or she has to lie."

"In my experience, both corporations and nonprofits can be untruthful in their lobbying efforts. And it isn't just about withholding damaging information. It's about actively presenting distorted or dishonest information. I worry that it has become appropriate in D.C. for lobbyists to flat-out lie."

"Manipulative techniques that are ineffective in lobbying members of Congress and their staffs may be quite effective in influencing public opinion."

VALUE CONSISTENCY

"In one of my earlier positions, my boss, who owned the firm, wanted me to go out and get new clients to represent that would bring in a lot of money. I wouldn't do that because of other values. So I went to work for another boss whose values were more consistent with my own. . . . People I've known who worked in the nonprofit sector and then went to work for big money lobbying firms or law firms dress a lot better, but they don't look happy. To some people in the field it becomes clear that over time they are going to wind up dealing with some things that, even if they didn't think they were downright unethical, they don't want to spend their life doing. I think this happens more often than people know, that folks go to work for lobbying firms and they don't like representing their client. So they go and try to find other clients. And if they can do that to bring in business, they stay. Otherwise they leave, or at least get their firms to let them do some pro bono work. Often I think what lobbyists do, they might not think it's wrong, it's just kind of soul-deadening. They go home and think of what they've accomplished in a week, thinking up a scheme of making 'X' better, so that the client's going to make a little more money or have less hassle and regulations. It doesn't work for a grown-up. And so people find a way to get some pro bono work on a lawsuit or lobbying campaign."

"I tell my potential clients that to succeed, they need to look for an intersection between their bottom line and society's interest."

"I know what my client wants; no one knows what the common good is."

"Have you ever heard of a lobbyist who declined a client because the CEO of the client firm says: 'We are not going to change [certain unethical] practices, that's not the issue here. I want you to kill that bill nonetheless'?"

"I've seen lots of times when young people don't agree with what the boss has been telling them, and yet they have to write talking points and a speech on a topic."

"Is politically effective lobbying always the same as ethically responsible lobbying?"

"I like my clients. I think my clients as individuals are good people, yet some of them are polluters. Their goal is to pay as little taxes as possible. They don't want to do anything unethical or illegal."

"When my children were little, they wouldn't tell anybody that their mother was a lobbyist. It didn't sound like such a good thing. But I have been lucky. I have always been able to find jobs lobbying for things I believe in."

"There's only one ethical issue that I see lobbyists really wrestling with, and that is the basic question of whether you want to represent a particular client."

"Once a lobbyist has taken a job, the lobbyist's job is to get done what the client wants. So you must check this sort of thing carefully in advance."

"Most of the things I have to lobby on, if there is a moral dilemma, I can't detect it."

PROFESSIONAL STANDARDS

"I would have to say a more systemic problem is a lack of professional definitions and standards for the lobbying profession as a whole—that's a systemic problem, along with the fact that you do not generally see self-policing or teaching an awareness of ethics."

"You have the ethical rules for lawyers. But how much do lawyers follow those in the way they're supposed to in this context [of lobbying]? I think this is not something that our profession has focused on seriously enough."

"Something like this [ethical guidelines] would be very helpful. It would be helpful just to identify for people where questions ought to be asked. As is true with a lot of lives, sometimes the important thing goes right by you and you don't even know it was important at the time."

"Law firms have standards on conflicts of interests between clients to guide us. This gives us some protection, but does not resolve the question of which client to accept and which to decline."

"The off-the-street lobbyist has a problem in that there is no one to turn to for advice or guidance, no institutional culture to instill a sense of what's unacceptable."

"I've worked at the local level, the state level, and the federal level, and the federal level is straighter than the state level, which is generally straighter than the local level."

"Anybody can be a lobbyist."

"Lobbying is a public profession. Should there be different professional obligations for lobbyists and lawyers?"

"There are limits to how much legal and moral codes can change moral expectations in a profession such as lobbying. The law can't take care of everything; what's missing in the current climate more than anything else is self-regulation."

"The fact that something's legal doesn't make it ethical."

"Most people in this field hardly give ethics a consideration."

"'Exploitation' is an ambiguous term. Is a company exploiting workers when it pays them less than they could receive from other employers in the same area?"

"Should a lobbyist be unwilling to work in coalition with some groups?"

"It is more effective for a lobbyist to present some of the issues on the other side. This allows you to preempt their arguments and these are likely to come out sometime anyway."

"I have seen growth in the presence of ethics officers in large corporations because the sentencing guidelines adopted in 1992 for certain criminal violations give credit to companies that have ethics officers."

"Yes, it happens all the time [that lobbyists are able to kill legislation]. . . . The situation is rarely posed so starkly. There are lots of ways to delay or modify legislation without outright trying to kill it, although such tactics may have the same effect."

"As a lobbyist, you take on an identification with your client and their issues."

"If you are going to represent one client in a matter that will be adverse to another client, you should tell them as a matter of professional courtesy."

"People in this business are close-mouthed when they have had ethical problems."

"Most paid lobbyists rarely get involved in direct moral questions like abortion."

"Regulations to prevent bribery are fine, but no one knows how to monitor fairness. No one knows exactly what that is."

CONFLICTS OF INTEREST

"I would argue that some firms are trying to get too many pieces of a limited pie, and they will be proportionally ineffective the more they take on. . . . If I'm trying to get as much as I can to do one side of a question it doesn't mean that I can do that if I'm getting $30 million to do otherwise. . . . They cannot represent so many conflicting interests, take on so much."

"In my independent lobbying firm, we turn down business all the time, but I don't put my job in jeopardy when I do so. Not so the director of governmental affairs of a company, who would probably be turning in a resignation if he or she decided that killing this bill was unethical."

"A potential client has a right to expect that you'll have 'the discussion' with them about possible conflicts of interest. In some places this might involve giving them your client list, but in a lot of other places it doesn't."

DISCLOSURE

"Disclosure in the lobbying area should be complete. People should not [have to] parse out whether a fee this hour was spent doing something that you shouldn't declare as lobbying, this [other] hour spent doing something that is lobbying. It all revolves around the same thing: advocacy. Maybe they should change the term, for the sake of the law, but I believe a system that disclosed all fees paid to advocate a position, whether they're public relations fees, government relations fees, whatever they are, and whatever branch of government, would be better disclosure and give people a better idea of what's going on."

"This was truly the undermining of transparency (in reference to the lobbying tactics used in the health care reform debate)."

REVOLVING DOOR

"Washington politics is an insider's game from which ordinary citizens are excluded. Players in the game move from policymaking roles to lobbying roles and vice versa."

"People are constantly leaving the hill to make money."

HIRED GUN AND VALUE NEUTRAL?

"Ethical issues exist at all levels. First of all, when you talk about the lobbyist, the lobbyist is simply a hired gun. Lobbyists have no principles. Lobbyists have no positions. You ask someone what do you think about this and he'll say I don't know, I don't have a client. We're sort of agnostics here. A client retains us, and that's fine, but if someone who didn't like that client retained us, well, that would be fine too. It's much like lawyers. You take the cases as presented to you. So lobbyists generally are very neutral on policy issues. If you raise the issue of ethics in lobbying, the first word that most people would respond with is 'money,' the enormous amount of money that flows through all sorts of channels, frequently undisclosed, in all kinds of ways, to influence legislative, regulatory, and judicial outcomes."

"Lobbyists have no positions, only clients."

"I confess to being a hired gun."

"A lobbyist is a hired gun and they are hired for a purpose—that's it."

USE OF THE MEDIA

"The slings and arrows in the arsenal of the lobbyist are many and generating spurious grass roots is one of them."

"You have media strategies that draw upon the grass roots, where firms increasingly spend millions of dollars to generate editorials and stories around the country. Is that generating influence in an unethical or false way? Congress might say, 'Oh, we don't respond to this,' but they do."

"It is important to distinguish between communication with political insiders and outsiders. Lobbyists, to be effective, need to preserve credibility with public officials and their staffs. But this need does not preclude the cynical manipulation of public opinion through political advertising. Respect for the insider may coexist with contempt for the outsider."

TREND TOWARD PUBLIC RELATIONS

"It's interesting to watch this . . . you're merging public relations and advertising with lobbying and government relations. Are there great similarities in what those do? Yes, there are. Are there different, very different, ethics involved in the doing of those things? The answer is yes. What I will look for is to see which one is influencing the other more. I have this fear that we'll see the advertising ethic become more the lobbying ethic. But if it does it will be sealing its own fate because it will be overstating and people will lose confidence. We'll see how that works out."

"In the public relations approach to lobbying, there is too much reliance on the use of half-truths, distortion, scare tactics, and misinformation."

CONFIDENTIALITY

"It's really important not to betray relationships and not to go behind a person's back or report to other people what that person said . . . but sometimes you go around them to a more senior person in the office, or to the member, when you can't get past a staff person, or that person is opposed to what you want and you know that that person is not sending the memos to the member reporting on our position. So if I do this, I feel I have to tell the person. I try not to give them so much warning that they can stop me. My style of lobbying is not to have big formal meetings, but to catch members on the fly as they're walking between the House and the office buildings."

UNJUSTIFIED OR UNEARNED FEES

"I think that [there are] lobbyists doing what I would consider to be unethical, charging $25,000 a month, and that is [the only activity]. This particular guy has no real contacts or clout in the area he's charging them for, he's ripping them off. Now, is that his fault? Is that unethical? One of the problems that I've seen recently is lobbyists will take set fees and don't do much of anything. I have problems with that. Or sometimes they lowball and say that the fee will be just $5,000 and all they do is raise [that fee] if you really get down to it."

THE ENDURING INFLUENCE OF LOBBYING ON AMERICAN DEMOCRACY

THE FUNCTIONING OF DEMOCRACY

"Well you know if you really push the ethical issue, if you want to push the ethical issue to the ultimate issue, it's really not the conduct of the lobbyists that's at issue so much as the functioning of democracy. There's certainly a moral issue at stake here. How are decisions made in a democracy? Ultimately it becomes the ethics of legislators rather than of lobbyists."

"We need to address unethical outcomes with systemic reform rather than focus on individual ethics."

"If people on the Hill are hearing from only one side on an issue, they have an affirmative duty to seek out the other voices, not the lobbyists. If a lobbyist made too strong a case for the other side, you would be suspicious of them."

"It's a two-way street. There might be a bunch of ethically shady lobbyists. But in a democratic society, all sorts of people get sent to serve in Congress, and you also have some in Congress who are morally bankrupt. In those cases, it's the lobbyists who are responsible for injecting morality into the whole situation."

"The carefully orchestrated campaign to defeat health care reform shows that our mental picture of the lobbying process is badly out of date."

"There's a fundamental ethical issue that maybe we all turn a blind eye to because we couldn't survive if we didn't. Most people want to play within the rules, but they're not sure the game itself is fair."

"The system is breaking down structurally. This process of decline is not covered by the press because it is not a conflict between two people."

"There are the voters, the party organization, and the party in government. That triangle's gotten weak everywhere, and what's taken its place? What's taken its place in terms of services to candidates are interest groups. They bring in money, volunteers, and therefore individualism in government grows rather than coming together in a commonality, because you've got all these . . . narrow focused groups putting pressure on members to get elected."

PUBLIC DISTRUST, CRITICS, AND REFORM

"The problem I've seen is that everybody's screaming 'murder.' That is not effective. A little bit of good won't do. If you're not going to do the perfect thing, they're going to call you a crook. I think they defeat themselves that way. You have people screaming 'murder.' But when something isn't murder, they ought to recognize it and take it. If I'm going to use an issue like this [lobbying reform] to raise money [for my organization] I've got to exaggerate it a little bit when I send out my mass mailings to get people to contribute."

REGULATION

"Unfortunately, Congress has chosen to regulate itself as if it were dishonest. We have a mindless system of regulations aimed at [appeasing] the critics, massive regulations to defend against criticism, that have nothing to do with conduct."

POLITICAL PARTICIPATION

"[As voting behavior is going down and lobbying behavior is going up] . . . something's being lost in the process. If you find the answer to that question, put it in the book. I think that's one of the toughest for the next generation. We have got to get people back involved in the political life of the country. . . . When people don't believe that the system is just, they don't want to be a part of it. So I think the answer, when it comes, will be that the competition to get people's ear or eye for a short period of time may actually result in a little more thoughtful critique of our system of government, which is outrageously good compared to many others."

"The real problem is that most people aren't involved politically and are not informed of what their government is doing."

A SLICE OF THE PIE

"It's my job to advance the interests of my association or client. Period."

"You are lobbying for a slice of the pie."

"I get annoyed with those who call for reform of the system, who proclaim that the special interests are taking over America. Well in my mind, every interest is special. If you're part of a group, you've got a special interest."

THE LEGISLATIVE SYSTEM

"Most bills are passed without anybody reading them. [Legislators] can't do it all in the time they've got. They have to spend too much time raising money for campaigns."

PUBLIC PERCEPTION OF LOBBYING

"Let's face it. As in any business there's a certain percentage of people out there who don't give a damn. Pardon me, but they don't care. They're going to do whatever they need to do to try to win. I don't know that there's any more of those people in the lobbying profession than anywhere else. Some really think 'lobbyist' is a dirty word. . . . Let's face it, not everybody, but a large percentage of the American public, is completely turned off to the [lobbying] process because they think it's corrupt. And some parts of the structure do have a tendency to move in that direction because of the money in the process. But the people who are here in my observation are for the most part very honest. . . . [Lobbyists] are not the corrupt group the people think they are. They have a job to do; most of them try to do it honestly and with some sense of what's right and wrong."

"In a democracy based on organized interest groups, the average person's views are left out of the mix."

INEQUALITIES OF POWER

"Lobbyists are not a constitutional part of the fabric of government. The legislature is. Modern processes are not geared to insure that all sides on an issue are effectively represented, and it would be wrong to blame that on the lobbyists."

"Some of the sophisticated tools of special interest lobbying, such as the artificial creation of grass roots opinion, etcetera, give unprecedented power to shape opinion."

"Significant inequalities of money and resources lead to inequalities of access and influence."

"The disproportionate resources available to the powerful create increasing political and economic inequalities."

"It isn't just money; the field is tilted toward any group that has an advantage of resources."

"Our dominant political ethics is 'don't penalize the strong to help the weak.' Make them do it themselves."

"That's the way the world works; the wealthy and well-organized can hire the best, most skilled advocates. That's an unfair part of the process. I don't see any way to change that."

POLITICAL STALEMATE

"What moves Washington is crisis or scandal, not theory or logic."

"Most lobbying is negative, to prevent the further extension of government power."

"Effective lobbying has the capacity to kill things before they get started."

CAPITALISM AND DEMOCRACY

"Does a corporation have an obligation to try to change the system in a foreign country if that country's system of laws permits 'exploitation'?"

"The market places limits on how far a company can go in being ethical if this increases costs."

"The corporation's obligation is to maximize returns to its shareholders. When it comes to foreign countries, corporations should not try to change the rules (in foreign countries) because other societies are entitled to their own values."

"Companies should only go beyond the law to the extent they need to maintain a stable workforce."

"If we individual lobbyists are limited by our personal ethical constraints, or if our organizations are so limited, we're then placed at a disadvantage, because the other side frequently knows no ethical bounds."

"The political system is democracy driven; the economic system is driven by wealth. There's always going to be a tension."

"Well, it presupposes some wise man who knows what the common good is. I don't see any obvious moral beacon here."

PUBLIC DISTRUST OF THE SYSTEM

"[The public has] a real fear of abuse of power and that somebody is out there doing bad things, special interests. And so the first thing they think about the lobbying profession [seems to be] 'that's bad.'"

"The tendency in our political culture is to construe public ethics narrowly."

CONCLUSIONS

As the preceding quotations make clear, the lobbyists whom we interviewed were exceptionally candid about the ethical challenges they and their colleagues confront in the course of their professional work. At the same time, many of them expressed uncertainty and confusion about the nature and objectivity of ethics and about the meaning and application of central ethical categories like justice and the common good. To address these concerns, this book includes a brief chapter on the purpose and method of ethics (chapter 2) and a longer chapter on the ethics of political advocacy (chapter 5).

After three years of careful study, we concluded that the practice of lobbying in the United States today raises two distinct kinds of ethical concerns. What we have called internal concerns arise for people directly engaged in the practice of lobbying, whether they are clients, lobbyists, or the public officials and their staffs whom they seek to influence. It is largely this type of concern that we sought to address in the Woodstock Principles (chapter 7). For several reasons, we did not endorse a substantive position on the intensely debated topic of campaign finance reform. We explicitly recognize, however, the tremendous role that money plays in American politics and the significant issues of political equity that the power of money raises. Until a fair and credible system of financing presidential and congressional elections is adopted, the ethical reform of lobbying will be incomplete. Now that the Bipartisan Campaign Reform Act of 2002 (commonly known as McCain-Feingold) has become law, we wait to see how effective it will be in improving electoral practice and restoring public trust.

The substantive issues we did address arose directly from our interviews and group discussions. They include: the evident tension between a political culture focused on satisfying the demands of well-organized, well-financed special interests and a civic politics actively devoted to identifying and acting in the long-term public interest; the ethically appropriate relations between lobbyists and clients, lobbyists and policymakers, and lobbyists and shapers of public opinion; conflicts of interest that arise for the practicing lobbyist; the important distinction between legitimate and improper lobbying strategies and tactics; and the evident need to enhance the integrity and reputation of the lobbying profession.

Systemic concerns about the influence of organized interests on the health of American democracy are harder to address in specific reforms. Yet, both active participants and critical observers agree that the negative perception of lobbyists by ordinary Americans has contributed to diminished public confidence in the electoral and decision-making process. Popular distrust of government has serious consequences for our democracy. It produces an alienated and disengaged citizenry, discourages public-spirited citizens from seeking political office, threatens the credibility of elected officials, and reduces the prospects for fair and farsighted policies and laws. It is a major hope of this study that an ethical reform of lobbying will promote greater public confidence in the procedural and substantive fairness of American political life.

A final ethical issue needs much greater public discussion: the complex interdependence of capitalism and democracy. A free-enterprise economy and democratic political institutions have coexisted in the United States since our founding in the late eighteenth century. The present study of lobbying presumes their continued coexistence in the new century. However, we need to acknowledge a manifest tension between the capitalist drive to maximize profits and shareholder return and the democratic political imperative to promote the enduring good of the national community, particularly of its weakest and most vulnerable citizens. The institutional separation of economic and political power and the clear cultural distinction between capitalist and democratic values are critically essential if the historic conjunction between capitalism and democracy is to be compatible with the American promise of liberty and justice for all.

We have identified the ethical challenges of lobbying—we have heard them described by practitioners in the field. Now let us examine the comprehensive moral framework within which we can understand and evaluate these challenges.

2 THE PURPOSE AND METHOD OF ETHICS

Although people frequently use the terms "ethical" and "moral," we rarely attempt to articulate what they mean. This chapter initiates that task of articulation by addressing two basic questions: "What is ethics?" and "How are conflicts among ethical judgments to be resolved?"[1]

Ethics is a form of practical inquiry; it is a matter of learning and doing. We are trying to discover something important, and we do not assume at the outset that we know precisely what we are seeking. That is why ethics, like science, begins by asking questions about our experience. But ethics is an explicitly practical inquiry. The conclusions that we reach on the basis of our ethical deliberations are conclusions that we must live by if we are going to preserve our personal and public integrity.

What are ethical debates about? They are about very basic and inescapable things: about the type of persons we should become; the kinds of communities we should create; about what we should do and avoid doing; about the rights and responsibilities of human beings; about the range of goods—social, economic, cultural, personal, and spiritual—that are necessary for human well-being; and about gradations of good and evil (why are some "goods" more important and some evils more dangerous than others?).

These debates do not occur in an historical vacuum. They are shaped by the moral traditions we have inherited and to which we still give some measure of allegiance. Four central traditions have shaped Western thinking about right and wrong, about good and evil. The fact that each tradition has a somewhat different ethical emphasis and uses a distinctive ethical vocabulary adds to the complexity of contemporary ethical discourse and argument.

The first tradition—one of the earliest, but one that still has great vitality today—is called "virtue ethics." This tradition starts with the ancient Greeks and is most fully developed by Aristotle. It holds that the heart of the ethical life is the cultivation and exercise of virtue. Virtues are the habits of character and intellect that human beings acquire in the course of their education and upbringing. These personal virtues, which are deliberately cultivated by a sound moral community, enable us to discover what is genuinely good, to discern what is wrong and harmful, and to develop the courage and consistency of character to act on our moral discoveries and insights.

The second important tradition, which is connected to the rule-oriented aspect of ethics, comes from Hebrew Scripture with its Law and Ten Commandments. The Commandments are a set of moral prescriptions, telling us how we ought to behave, and moral prohibitions, commanding us not to act in certain ways. The striking thing about the ancient biblical Commandments is their extraordinary staying power. Here is an ethical code, formulated by a nomadic people under very trying historical circumstances, that continues to serve us well in our personal and public lives.

Because of our moral traditions, we do not have to reinvent the ethical wheel. We already know that certain things are wrong, such as stealing, lying. and killing. However, even though the biblical Commandments are exceptionally direct ("Thou shalt not kill"), it is not always clear what they practically entail. Take the prohibition against murder, for example. What does it imply concretely about fighting in war, about self-defense, about capital punishment? General ethical guidelines can be clear, but their application to specific cases is often a matter of dispute. There is a dimension of uncertainty in the interpretation of moral rules that the rules themselves cannot resolve. That is one reason why laws and rules need to be connected to virtues, why the prescription and prohibition of actions need to be complemented by the moral agent's excellence of intellect and character. In ethics, both *what* we do, and *why* and *how* we do it, are of critical importance.

The prophetic tradition is the third significant part of our ethical inheritance. The Hebrew prophets were regularly persecuted for speaking truth to those in power and for challenging the moral complacency of their community. Prophets tend to be without honor in their own country because the truths they voice are often unwelcome. They speak on behalf of the poor and the powerless, the widow and the orphan. They insist that a just society is finally measured by how well it provides for the least advantaged, for immigrants, children, the elderly, the disabled, the emotionally disturbed. In a capitalistic society like ours—constantly focused on success, profits, reputation, and power—the prophetic voice, with its emphasis on the needs and concerns of the least of our brothers and sisters, is an especially important source of justice.

Fourth is the democratic tradition in ethics, which we take for granted today. Yet, it is really striking, when one studies European history before the democratic revolutions of the eighteenth century, how different the prevailing assumptions were then. It was simply assumed that there were different levels of society, whose members lived under different laws, enjoyed different rights and privileges, and were born with radically different expectations and prospects. In the United States today, we start from the presumption of individual equality: equality under the law, equality of rights and responsibilities, equality of voice in resolving disputed public questions, and concrete equality of opportunity in the pursuit of a meaningful life. The burden of proof in a democratic society is on any person, group, or institutional practice that violates these norms of democratic equality.

Real progress is made in the history of ethics. We do not constantly need to return to square one. It is no longer an issue in our society, for instance, that racial discrimination is wrong. It took us a long, bloody struggle to recognize this contested truth and we are still engaged in correcting the effects of racism. But the basic point has been made and accepted. The same could be said about the denial of religious liberty, the unequal treatment of men and women, and the pollution of the natural and human environment. We know that these historical practices are wrong and should be effectively ended.

Now these important moral truths are not self-evident. If they had been, our ancestors would have known that these were unjust and unacceptable ways of treating other people. Rather, over the course of time, by reflecting on human experience, by observing the patterns of history, by taking everyone's perspective into account, we have gradually discovered that many things are wrong and unfair.

We have also discovered much that is humanly good. A sound education for all children is good; so is a healthy and pleasing environment, a safe place to live, an adequate balance of work and leisure, and a legally guaranteed set of rights and liberties. It is true that human goods often conflict. That is why we need to determine their order of importance and urgency. It is also true that rights may conflict. These instances of legitimate conflict create the difficult calls in ethical decision making. In dealing with moral conflict, we need to make sure that everyone who is going to be affected by the anticipated decision has a meaningful voice in the deliberative process. Equitable decision-making procedures are fundamental to democratic fairness and sustainable practical outcomes.

The existence of a plurality of goods, rights, and interests forces us to confront the central notion of public ethics, the notion of the "common good." In practical inquiry, the common good serves as a heuristic rather than a substantive category. That is to say, it is not some specific and determinate thing we know in advance (substantive). The common good is what we are actively trying to discover (heuristic), to determine concretely and practically, in the course of political deliberation and debate.

One helpful way of thinking about the common good is to use a microcosmic example. If one takes a microcosmic community like the family, there are legitimate goods and rights that properly belong to the parents, the children, the grandparents, and—taking the long view—the ancestors and those yet to be born. Any approach to family decision making that privileges one of these groups to the significant disadvantage of others is morally wrong. This principle accounts for the ethical limitations of patriarchy, which unduly elevates the father of the family to the detriment of the mother and the children.

When one extends the requirement of common justice to a larger society, it naturally becomes more complicated. But the basic moral intuition remains in force. Everyone's rights are equal; everyone should have an equal opportunity to lead a good life; because of differences of ability and training, individuals will perform different public functions, but everyone should be treated with equal dignity and respect. If the result of a public policy, for example, is that it supports racial discrimination, or unduly burdens the poor, or leaves children unprotected, or violates civil liberties, or creates unjust distribution of social benefits and burdens, or threatens the environment, then we know that it is wrong and must be opposed.

Political deliberation and debate are always conducted in a moral and historical context. There are certain truths we already know, certain questions that we as a people have resolved, and there is much that remains to be settled and amended in the course of our common life. In a democratic society, the discovery and enactment of the common good requires an open and equitable process of deliberation and decision making; it also requires that the concrete outcomes that flow from public policy be just; that these policies help to create a more perfect civic union, establish distributive justice, ensure domestic tranquility, provide for the general defense, promote the general welfare, and secure the blessings of liberty for present and future generations.

In appraising a democratic society, from the perspective of the common good, we are attentive to both the deliberative process and its substantive outcomes. Are the legitimate concerns and opinions of all citizens equally represented in public debate? Are the benefits and burdens of public cooperation fairly distributed? Are greater goods given priority over lesser goods? Are individual rights and public responsibilities combined in the appropriate balance? Have we met our fiduciary obligations to posterity? Have we adequately considered the "widow" and the "orphan"? And is the well-being of the whole community adequately protected against concentrations of economic and political power?

At both the personal and public levels then, ethics is a fallible, self-correcting, multi-voiced process of trying to determine what is good and what is not, what is fair and not, what is right and not, and what truly respects the dignity of human beings and what does not. This is a normative deliberative process in which we all regularly engage. To maintain our personal integrity and to promote the well-being of our country, we need to think, choose, and act as well as we can. To live attentively, intelligently, reasonably, and responsibly, those are the perennial challenges of ethics.

Ethics, then, has direct and immediate relevance to the field of lobbying. The chief political truth that democracy teaches is that all citizens whose lives are affected by public decisions should have a meaningful voice in public debate. This truth is absolutely critical to the legitimate practice of lobbying. The purpose of lobbying reform is not to penalize citizens already engaged in the policymaking process, but to find adequate ways to extend and enhance the range of civic opinion that is actually heard and heeded.

NOTE

1. For the purposes of this chapter, we shall treat ethics and morality as equivalent concepts. The linguistic roots of both notions are classical. In ancient Greece, *ethike*, from which the English term "ethics" derives, meant habits; in classical Latin, *mores*, the etymological source of "morality," meant customs. Classical virtue ethics was chiefly concerned with the *ethike*, the habits that people acquired in the process of their personal formation and upbringing. When Greek concepts were translated into Latin, *ethike* became *mores*, the acquired virtues that were required for achieving the good human life. A modern ethical tradition, deriving from Immanuel Kant, assumes a sharper separation than we do between morality (our obligations to other persons) and ethics (the best way for a person to live).

3 THE STATE OF LOBBYING TODAY—AND RELATED ETHICAL QUESTIONS

IN AN INTERVIEW, A PROMINENT LOBBYIST RECENTLY REFLECTED ON THE PROFESSION:

Lobbying has changed a great deal since I started. When I started you needed to know two dozen people in all of Washington and you could be effective. That's who made the decisions. If you had the right associations, the right jobs, you probably knew them and could be successful. The post-Watergate era has evolved so that power is very diffuse. Everybody on the Hill is powerful in one area or another now. The administration is so much larger, just people-wise, so that it really involves an awful lot of educational work, public relations, making people aware of what people think back home. And the most important part of anything [now] is your strategy.

When you get to the end today it's just very, very different. You have to figure nearly every issue has an opponent. So, you're advocating one thing, another person is advocating another thing. And members try to be insulated from a process that would make them too subject to any one relationship influencing their vote. So it's really today very much a question of building coalitions and educating people and of creating a context for people to decide to be with you. If you can create public opinion for your point of view, it's much easier for a member to choose to be with you. And the days of choosing to be with you because, "Hey, good old Bill," . . . it's much less likely to happen. And if you're going to be an enduring business over a long period of time, you have to keep picking new people to become your best friend, or you have to become very substantive and have a lot of opinion shaping ability, because the people keep changing.

DEFINITIONS

This chapter seeks to provide an overview of what current social science has to say about lobbying the federal government. At the end of this restricted survey, we will discuss some implications of current practice for our basic questions about the ethics of lobbying.

We understand lobbying to be the deliberate attempt to influence political decisions through various forms of public advocacy. The lobbyist uses several means—such as personal reputation, professional obligation, cultivated rapport, and financial inducement—to gain the trust of public officials and their staffs and to achieve selected political goals. Lobbyists pursue their objectives either through "earned" access, by which the lobbyist can share information and opinions that influence the formation of public policy, or through "positional" influence, which is based on one's standing in the public realm rather than "earned" through other means.[1]

Every U. S. citizen may be a lobbyist in the broadest sense of the term, because the First Amendment to the U.S. Constitution establishes "the right of the people . . . to petition the Government for a redress of grievances." There are at present no clear technical guidelines defining the profession of lobbying. For example, there is no accrediting mechanism for lobbyists analogous to those that exist in the medical and legal professions. As a matter of fact, many—probably most—professionals who are involved in lobbying are not technically registered as lobbyists but still conform to the requirements of the law. Current U.S. law provides only a minimalist definition of who must register as a lobbyist, and the actual number of people who are professionally involved in lobbying is far larger than the number of people officially registered as lobbyists.

Our study focuses exclusively on lobbying the federal government in Washington, D.C. The major actors involved in lobbying are *clients* (individual persons or organized interests) who may contract with *lobbyists* (individuals, other departments of the client firm, or outside firms) who then develop various methods, strategies, and tactics (e.g., through a lobbying campaign design) to inform, influence, and pressure *policymakers* (e.g., legislators or executive branch administrators and their staffs) who make policy decisions that inevitably will affect the well-being of the *public*, that is, the common good of the American people. Interest group lobbying may be undertaken directly through trade association or union representation, or through special interest group representatives in Washington. There also is a type of surrogate representation by "guns for hire," who might be lawyer-lobbyists, participants in multiple-client firms that specialize in lobbying, or part of one of the new "megafirms" that combine lobbying, public relations, and government relations.[2]

Although some of these participants in the deliberative process may consider themselves formally as "lobbyists," many others, e.g., the average citizen at home, also undertake such activities directly or indirectly without considering or defining themselves as lobbyists.

HISTORY

Some form of what we presently call lobbying is as old as politics itself. The right to petition government, present in codes as early as the *Magna Carta* (June 15, 1215), has a long history in the Western legal tradition.[3] At the inception of the U.S. system of constitutional government, James Madison, in *Federalist Papers* 10, argued for a strong federal union based on popular representation as the appropriate "republican remedy" for combating factions—organized interest groups that threaten the public good.[4] Under U.S. law, lobbying is a protected exercise of the people's right to petition their government for the redress of grievances.

In the nineteenth century, there were no specific legal guidelines for lobbying the federal government. Gifts and other explicit quid pro quos could flow openly without shame between lobbyist and policymaker. Today, explicit legal codes in the executive[5] and legislative[6] branches of government severely limit direct transfers between lobbyists and federal office holders. The next chapter of this book gives an overview of these legal codes as they currently exist.

Despite considerable journalistic probing in recent years, the ethical challenges of lobbying have not received much attention in the professional literature. One observer maintains that "ethics in the lobbying business have improved dramatically over the past four decades, not because of legislative edicts and regulation, but because of the quality of the members of Congress, the quality of the lobbyists, and the dispersion of power away from the Sam Rayburn prototype to something close to a 'one-person one-vote' regime in Congress."[7] But Elizabeth Drew challenges such assertions in her book *The Corruption of American Politics: What Went Wrong and Why*[8]; she maintains that the quality of American politicians has clearly declined since Watergate.

DEVELOPMENTS IN LOBBYING, 1960–2000

Our opening quotation for this chapter, from a prominent lobbyist, touches on many of the recent developments in the field. We discuss here some further trends in lobbying in the period 1960–2000, as described by journalists and political scientists. In the past forty years, the rapidly expanding number of interest groups involved in lobbying have centralized their efforts in Washington. Some of these groups deal with the public interest and the overall quality of our political life, but many others have a narrow focus, often on a single advocacy issue. Although the number of public interest groups involved in federal lobbying has grown, such citizens' groups constitute only a small fraction of the total lobbying effort in Washington. "As the number of [interest] groups soars, the relative power of all groups declines."[9] Corporate interests are said to represent as much as 60 percent of the lobbying activities in Washington.

Lobbying interests have developed far more sophisticated, timely, and specialized political strategies to accomplish their goals.[10] New electronic technologies are having a tremendous impact on the speed, quantity, and targeting of public policy advocacy. A great deal of political commentary—and a bit much less legislative action—has focused on campaign finances, the expansion of soft money, and political action committees funded by special interests.[11] Although political participation in the United States is on the decline, especially among the poor and lower middle class,[12] and political parties seem to be losing their traditional clout, lobbying interests are expanding rapidly, gaining more access and influence. An increased amount of lobbying is being done by nongovernmental organizations—such as educational institutions, foundations, and churches—as well as by state, local, and foreign governments. Lobbying is both devolving to state and local political centers and expanding to global institutions such as the United Nations. With congressional power so evenly divided between the two major parties, lobbying firms and coalitions are becoming more and more diverse and bipartisan in their memberships and in their selection of routes to the formation of policy. In fact, the reliance on lobbying coalitions has become increasingly important in recent years.

No branch of government, not even the judiciary, seems to be untouched by the direct and indirect influence of special economic and political interests. Whether the relationships lobbying creates be described as iron triangles joining lobbyists, executives, and legislators or as more complex "sloppy large hexagons," lobbying in Washington is pervasive. Political scientist Ronald Shaiko identifies the following connections between lobbyists and the agencies of the federal government:[13] the *electoral connection,* involving the relationships among interest groups, political action committees, and campaigns;[14] the *congressional connection,* through inside strategies, such as providing sometimes highly technical information to policymakers and outside grassroots strategies and tactics;[15] the *executive connection,* through which presidents and cabinet officials more and more function as lobbyists and as receivers of lobbying efforts; and the *judicial connection,* through which—though overt lobbying of judges may be very rare and often counterproductive, leading to a justice removing himself or herself from a case—interest groups and lobbyists use many other ways to influence the judicial branch (e.g., through educational programs and advertising campaigns artificially generating public opinion, by attempting to influence the selection of judges through hearings during the nomination process, and by setting the judicial agenda through campaigns of litigation).[16]

POLITICAL CHANGES, 1960–2000

These notable developments in lobbying parallel many significant political changes on the Washington scene. In the past forty years, there has been significant growth in the size, power, and responsibilities of the federal government. At the same time, Franklin D. Roosevelt's New Deal coalition has completely dissolved. The political power of organized labor has weakened, due to a significant decline in union membership, particularly as a percentage of the total workforce. Largely as a result of federal civil rights legislation, the once "solid South" became heavily Republican, whereas many poorer central cities are governed by black Democrats. The earlier traditional loyalty of immigrant and ethnic Catholics to the Democratic Party has greatly weakened.

There has been an unprecedented political mobilization of corporate interests, and the coming of a heightened sophistication within the business lobby. These corporate initiatives have developed in response to consumer advocacy, the environmental movement, the legislative and regulatory initiatives of the Great Society, and the counterforce of organized labor. Globalization of the economy has led to a marked emphasis on corporate reorganization, cost cutting, and downsizing. Significant changes in the American class structure have been caused by the emergence of a service-oriented, postindustrial society. It is now far more difficult for unskilled labor to earn a living wage, and a much higher premium is placed on education and skills in the workforce. Benefits coverage has declined for many workers, especially in the growing service sector. Changes in the family structure (divorce, out of wedlock births, etc.) have increased the social welfare burden of the government, but such welfare benefits are less secure than in the past.

In this same period, there has been a tremendous increase in the cost of financing political campaigns. Elected public officials must be constantly involved in the pursuit of campaign money, much of which is provided by organized interests that also have lobbying objectives. The reduced influence of political parties means that they are less able to perform the electoral and policy-related activities that they used to provide for their chosen candidates. Many of these policy-development activities are now performed by lobbyists or special interest groups, which at times actually draft the legislation to be voted upon. The rapidly spinning "revolving door" between government and the lobbying world implies an increased penetration of political and economic interests into the corridors of power: The White House, Congress, and regulatory agencies both receive and spin off people highly experienced in the world of lobbying.

IDEOLOGICAL SHIFT

Since the 1960s, there has been a significant shift to the right in Congress, the presidency, and the courts. Some contributing factors include an aggressive, heavily financed, and well-publicized conservative ideology that is hostile to big government and supportive of unregulated market competition. Conservative think tanks, intellectuals, and their political allies challenge the legitimacy of the welfare state and promote the economic advantages of privatization. A complex but effective electoral alliance has been forged between economic conservatives favoring lower taxes and reduced governmental power and social conservatives outraged by what they view as permissiveness and decadence in U.S. manners and morals.

Even within the Democratic Party, the power of unions and urban political machines has declined, while the power of the intellectual and technological elites with less of a commitment to social justice and economic equality has increased. There have also been important demographic changes, with population shifts from cities to suburbs, from the North and East to the South and West, as well as substantial Hispanic immigration to the United States. During the past forty years, the risk of governmental stalemate on matters of major national concern has increased. An increasingly partisan politics is driven by opposing ideologies. "We now have a more contentious interest group environment [in Washington]. . . . Now [many interest] groups are more closely identified with one party and one ideology than at any time in the recent past."[17]

PROFESSIONAL ISSUES

Although groups such as the American League of Lobbyists[18] have developed a code of ethics for lobbying, the profession still needs clearer standards and more reliable self-monitoring. Many lobbyists whom we have consulted for this project agree that the development of greater ethical awareness and higher standards of conduct are crucial for the credibility and advancement of their profession.

There are many other professional organizations whose members are involved in lobbying, such as the American Bar Association, American Association of Political Consultants, American Society of Association Executives, National Association of Business Political Action Committees, Public Affairs Council, and Women in Government Relations. There is clearly a need for further ethical reflection on lobbying activities, and on the connection between lobbyists' ethical codes and responsible practice.

PUBLIC DISTRUST

A recent national survey on what kind of government people in the United States want reveals a significant amount of dissatisfaction with the perceived role of interest group politics. An open-ended question asked, "What bothers you most about U.S. politics?" The leading answer was "Involve the general public more" and the next was "Cut the bureaucracy," but close behind in third place was "Get rid of lobbying/interest groups" (a little more than 11 percent of all those who responded). More specifically, the survey asked if people thought "interest groups should be prohibited from contacting members of Congress." An amazing 45.5 percent of all respondents nationwide agreed or strongly agreed with this statement. "Special interests have too much control of what government does." Just short of 80 percent agreed with this statement; many of these were "strongly agrees." Similarly, when asked whether or not various parts of government had too much power, about the right amount of power, or not enough power, more than 71 percent said that "interest groups have too much power" and only 8.4 percent said that they had "not enough power."[19]

Lobbying's tattered image: Is it deserved? It seems that only the most egregious cases (e.g., presidential pardons, illegal fund-raising) receive critical attention. For the most part, there is widespread public ignorance about the actual conduct of political advocacy and its causal effects on American democracy. And the little the American public knows about lobbying does not give the profession much credibility. Would increased public understanding of what lobbyists actually do and heightened ethical standards among lobbyists themselves significantly enhance their professional reputation?

ETHICAL QUESTIONS

There are many critical books by journalists[20] and political scientists[21]—as well as regular columns in the Washington press[22]—that monitor lobbying. Most of these, however—especially the journalistic treatments—do not probe beyond particular incidents. Monitoring services and newsletters such as *Influence Online*, *Federal Ethics Report*, and the *Ethics in Government Reporter* and watchdog groups such as the *Congressional Accountability Project*, the *Center for Responsive Politics*, the *Center for Public Integrity*, and *Common Cause* at times delve more deeply into conflicts of interest, but they rarely touch upon basic systemic issues such as how lobbying relates to the common good. Our interviews and group meetings with many lobbyists have identified some of the deeper ethical questions that need to be addressed, leading to a more comprehensive institutional monitoring of lobbying practice.[23]

Our listing of some of these concerns, which flow from our consultations with lobbyists, is by no means comprehensive. The following concerns, which will be examined more fully in chapter 5, provide examples of the types of issues we will be developing in chapter 7 as we recommend ethical principles for lobbying.

Do politically effective lobbying and ethically responsible lobbying sometimes diverge? There may at times be a profound tension between the professional and civic responsibilities of lobbyists. How can these tensions be resolved, doing justice to both sources of personal obligation?

Are ordinary citizens too often excluded from Washington politics because it is an insider's game, largely controlled by the revolving door among government, corporate, and lobbying positions? Are current regulations dealing with the revolving door sufficient? How can "outsiders" gain sufficient information and access to make their positions known within the policymaking process?

In many cases, we still lack full disclosure of the clients a lobbyist represents, or of the actual funding sources for grassroots and public relations campaigns. Is this consistent with the responsible exercise of democratic liberties? Should not the right to petition government include an obligation of transparency about who is advocating which positions to whom, and who is paying for that advocacy?

The growing public relations and advertising mentality in lobbying threatens greater reliance on half-truths, distortion, scare tactics, and misinformation in pursuing political goals. Is there any way to require "truth in advertising" in such situations? Manipulative techniques may be ineffective in lobbying members of Congress and their staffs, but such distortions often prove highly effective in influencing public opinion. Is reliance on such cynical techniques consistent with the purposes and principles of democracy?

Significant inequalities of money and resources among those lobbying a particular issue lead to inequalities of access and influence. Is there any way to enhance every citizen's right to effective representation so that all positions on an issue are seriously considered?

Recently, DeLancy W. Davis, vice president of the lobbying firm Jolly/Rissler Incorporated and a prominent lobbyist himself, claimed: "Our profession is fundamentally changing. We're moving toward a much more antiseptic, more fact-based type of lobbying. . . . The days of going to a chairman and cutting a deal are over."[24] What are the political and ethical implications of this change, and what alternative routes to political influence will now be pursued? Will such alternative strategies be more or less open to democratic influence?

Given Shaiko's argument that lobbying now affects every branch of government, ethical issues touch on these several connections, as well as on their effect on the "separation of powers" long considered to be an essential aspect of our constitutional system. Is the pervasiveness and penetration of lobbying now blurring these lines even further? Perhaps a new threshold of ethical and boundary questions for lobbyists and executives occurred with the numerous questionable pardons in the last hours of Bill Clinton's administration. These developments obviously demand ethical reflection about the presumed "immunity" of the courts from lobbying activity.

The fact that coalitions have become increasingly important in lobbying means that deeper ethical reflection on how these coalitions actually work is needed. For example, what are the trade-offs required when one issue becomes part of a coalition's larger "package" of issues in a specific lobbying campaign? What are the ethical limits beyond which a coalition member should not go in collaborative political advocacy? How is a lobbyist to determine these limits?[25]

Trade associations and other umbrella organizations are becoming more and more involved in lobbying. Professional ethical norms for these types of advocacy groups are called for, especially when the staff of such organizations themselves become the principal spokespersons in a given coalition.

The fact that lobbying often has its ultimate impact through interventions in the mark-up period of congressional legislation highlights the increased importance of legislative committee structures and the need to track the influences shaping legislation from start to finish. What does it mean for American democracy when lobbyists virtually become the authors of pieces of legislation? What does it mean when last-minute amendments and trade-offs end up being the basis of some of our most important social policies affecting the common good?

What are the limits of legal and ethical codes in changing moral expectations and conduct? Though the most recent (1995–2000) legal regulations of lobbying in the executive and legislative branches put severe restrictions upon gifts and political fundraising, and require examination of conflicts of interest and fuller disclosure, there remain important ethical issues not covered by existing legal codes. Perhaps the greatest of these issues has to do with the relationship between lobbying and the integrity and credibility of the democratic process.

One of our interviewees said: "There's a fundamental ethical issue that maybe we all turn a blind eye to because we couldn't survive if we didn't. Most people want to play within the rules, but they're not sure the game itself is fair." Since the mid-1960s, there has been a marked decline of public confidence in the integrity of the electoral and decision-making process. Public cynicism about government has serious consequences; it negatively affects citizen participation at all levels, subverts the perceived legitimacy of public officials, and reduces the prospects for effective political reform. The visible power of organized interest groups intensifies the troubling shift from civic to claimant politics.

The dominant role of money in American politics raises the suspicion that politics is becoming a "pay-to-play" system. Getting your share of the public pie becomes the principal motive for political activity. A politics dominated by organized interest groups leads to civic fragmentation and the loss of a national moral community. Skepticism about the common good, about the long-term well-being of the entire national community, becomes pervasive. If politics is becoming exclusively the pursuit of private interests, then appeals to the common good ring increasingly hollow. Radical inequalities of economic and political power become mutually reinforcing (deep pockets speak). The needs and concerns of the poor and powerless are systematically disadvantaged. This pattern of reinforcing power that favors the privileged is particularly disturbing to those religious and secular communities that emphasize a preferential option for the poor and disadvantaged.

The decline in electoral participation coinciding with the dramatic growth in lobbying raises ominous questions for American democracy. Is there a causal connection between the decrease in voting and the increase in lobbying activity, or is there merely a correlation in these discernible political trends? In either case, a disengaged and embittered electorate threatens the future of our democratic experiment.

Some of the most crucial questions are about procedural and distributive justice: Is national policy formed in a fair and responsible manner? Is the existing distribution of public benefits and burdens just? The practice of lobbying highlights a structural tension between the economic values of free-market capitalism (efficiency, profit, competition) and the political values of a democratic republic (equal liberty and justice for all). Unregulated capitalism inevitably heightens economic inequality, which over time deepens political inequality. The opinions, interests, and concerns of the powerful become far more influential than those of the poor and the middle class. These structural issues highlight the serious limitations of a political society founded exclusively on the pursuit of self-interest. Such a system proves ineffective in addressing serious and enduring national problems that affect the well-being of all citizens. Contemporary examples include radical economic inequality; reasonable entitlement reforms; a fair and efficient health financing and delivery system; the deteriorating condition of American cities; the quality of public education; and the financing of electoral campaigns.

In summary, the essential elements of lobbying have more and more complex ethical implications. Lobbyists' gaining access; creating trust; building relationships; generating public support or resistance; and accurately conveying information, analysis, and policy recommendations—all these inherently political activities require deeper ethical reflection than is provided by current legal and professional codes.

The most basic normative questions remain for those engaged in and concerned about the lobbying profession. What does lobbying actually contribute to the policy formation process? What political goods does it advance? What public harm does it cause? Is lobbying as currently practiced in Washington really consistent with Madison's view of competing factions effectively checking each other's influence within a republican form of government? Who are the regular winners and losers in this interest-driven process? How does lobbying protect the needs and rights of the voiceless, and of the ordinary citizens who have no interest groups to plead their cause? These, then, are among the pressing ethical issues we will examine in the following chapters of this book.

NOTES

1. We owe some of this terminology to the work of William T. Murphy, Jr., derived from our interview with him on May 14, 1999, when he was director of the Lobbying Institute of the Center for Congressional and Presidential Studies at American University's School of Public Affairs in Washington.

2. Paul S. Herrnson, Ronald G. Shaiko, and Clyde Wilcox, eds., *The Interest Group Connection: Electioneering, Lobbying, and Policymaking in Washington* (Chatham, N.J.: Chatham House Publishers, 1998), 4–10.

3. For a fuller history of lobbying, see James Deakin, *The Lobbyists* (Washington, D.C.: Public Affairs Press, 1966), chap. 3.

4. As Madison stated: "AMONG the numerous advantages promised by a well constructed Union, none deserves to be more accurately developed than its tendency to break and control the violence of faction. . . .

   "Complaints are everywhere heard from our most considerate and virtuous citizens, equally the friends of public and private faith, and of public and personal liberty, that our governments are too unstable, that the public good is disregarded in the conflicts of rival parties, and that measures are too often decided, not according to the rules of justice and the rights of the minor party, but by the superior force of an interested and overbearing majority. . . ." These [distresses] must be chiefly, if not wholly, effects of the unsteadiness and injustice with which a factious spirit has tainted our public administrations. . . . By a faction, I understand a number of citizens, whether amounting to a majority or a minority of the whole, who are united and actuated by some common impulse of passion, or of interest, adversed to the rights of other citizens, or to the permanent and aggregate interests of the community. . . .

"There are two methods of curing the mischiefs of faction: the one, by removing its causes; the other, by controlling its effect. There are again two methods of removing the causes of faction: the one, by destroying the liberty which is essential to its existence; the other, by giving to every citizen the same opinions, the same passions, and the same interests. It could never be more truly said than of the first remedy, that it was worse than the disease. Liberty is to faction what air is to fire, an aliment without which it instantly expires. But it could not be less folly to abolish liberty, which is essential to political life, because it nourishes faction, than it would be to wish the annihilation of air, which is essential to animal life, because it imparts to fire its destructive agency. The second expedient is as impracticable as the first would be unwise. . . . The regulation of these various and interfering interests forms the principal task of modern legislation, and involves the spirit of party and faction in the necessary and ordinary operations of the government. . . . "It is in vain to say that enlightened statesmen will be able to adjust these clashing interests, and render them all subservient to the public good. Enlightened statesmen will not always be at the helm. . . . The inference to which we are brought is, that the CAUSES of faction cannot be removed, and that relief is only to be sought in the means of controlling its EFFECTS. . . . From this view of the subject it may be concluded that a pure democracy, by which I mean a society consisting of a small number of citizens, who assemble and administer the government in person, can admit of no cure for the mischiefs of faction. . . .

"A republic, by which I mean a government in which the scheme of representation takes place, opens a different prospect, and promises the cure for which we are seeking. . . . The influence of factious leaders may kindle a flame within their particular States, but will be unable to spread a general conflagration through the other States. A religious sect may degenerate into a political faction in a part of the Confederacy; but the variety of sects dispersed over the entire face of it must secure the national councils against any danger from that source. A rage for paper money, for an abolition of debts, for an equal division of property, or for any other improper or wicked project, will be less apt to pervade the whole body of the Union than a particular member of it; in the same proportion as such a malady is more likely to taint a particular county or district, than an entire State. In the extent and proper structure of the Union, therefore, we behold a republican remedy for the diseases most incident to republican government. And according to the degree of pleasure and pride we feel in being republicans, ought to be our zeal in cherishing the spirit and supporting the character of Federalists." The quotation is taken from *The Federalist, by Alexander Hamilton, James Madison, and John Jay*, ed. Benjamin Fletcher Wright (Cambridge, Mass.: Belknap Press of Harvard University Press, 1961), 129–36.

5. U.S. Office of Government Ethics, "Standards of Ethical Conduct for Employees of the Executive Branch" <www.usoge.gov/pages/laws_regs_fedreg_stats/oge_regs/5cfr2635.html>, March 17, 1999.

6. U.S.C. 1605, "Lobbying Disclosure Act, Public Law 104-65, 104th Congress" <http://clerkweb.house.gov/pd/lobby/pl/10465.pdf>.

7. Hernnson, Shaiko, and Wilcox, Interest Group Connection, 34.

8. Elizabeth Drew, *The Corruption of American Politics: What Went Wrong and Why* (New York: McGraw Hill, 1999).

9. Thomas E. Patterson, *The Vanishing Voter: Public Involvement in an Age of Uncertainty* (New York: Knopf, 2002), in press.

10. Haynes Johnson and David S. Broder, *The System: The American Way of Politics at the Breaking Point* (Boston: Little, Brown, 1996), 194–224.

11. Allan J. Cigler and Burdett A. Loomis, *Interest Group Politics*, 5th edition (Washington, D.C.: CQ Press, 1998), 1–2.

12. Shorenstein Center, Harvard University, "Vanishing Voter Project."

13. Hernnson, Shaiko, and Wilcox, Interest Group Connection, 16–17.

14. Ibid., 37–51.

15. Ibid., 89–99.

16. Ibid., 267–88.

17. Ibid., 212.

18. American League of Lobbyists, "Code of Ethics" <www.alldc.org/ethicscode.htm>.

19. Correspondence with John Hibbing, University of Nebraska–Lincoln, based on the Gallup poll data collected for his forthcoming book (coauthored by Elizabeth Theiss-Morse), *Stealth Democracy: How Americans Want Government to Work* (New York: Cambridge University Press, 2002).

20. Jeffrey H. Birnbaum, *The Lobbyists: How Influence Peddlers Work Their Way in Washington* (New York: Times Books, 1992).

21. Ken Silverstein, *Washington on $10 Million a Day* (Monroe, Maine: Common Courage Press, 1998).

22. "Special Interests," Judy Sarasohn's column on lobbying and its influence on, government runs Thursdays on the *Washington Post's* Federal Page.
23. See chapter 2 above for a discussion of the aims, process, and terminology of ethics.
24. Bill McAllister, "Column," *Washington Post,* Jan. 27, 1998: A15.
25. Kevin W. Hula, *Lobbying Together: Interest Group Coalitions in Legislative Politics* (Washington, D.C.: Georgetown University Press, 1999).

4 FEDERAL REGULATION OF LOBBYING

The practice of lobbying at the federal level is subject to various types of regulation. The practice also enjoys constitutional protection. Without attempting to cover the field exhaustively, this chapter offers a brief survey of the constitutional issues raised by lobbying regulation, the principal federal statutes regulating lobbying and campaign finance, and the administrative regime that monitors and regulates lobbying and campaign finance.

One cannot get a full picture of how the law restricts lobbying simply by looking at the lobbying laws alone, particularly the Federal Regulation of Lobbying Act of 1995. Lobbyists and their clients must also heed other federal statutes—including provisions of the Internal Revenue Code and the criminal statutes banning bribery and gratuities—as well as advisory opinions of government ethics boards. In addition, various laws regulating the financing of federal election campaigns—which remain a perennial subject of public debate—also limit the types of strategies that may be used in the effort to influence lawmakers.

LOBBYING REGULATION

LOBBYING DISCLOSURE ACT OF 1995

Although lobbying in one form or another is as old as the Republic, direct federal statutory regulation of the practice did not begin until Congress enacted the Federal Regulation of Lobbying Act of 1946.[1] From that point until the present, the principal mechanism for regulation has been disclosure—public reporting of the lobbyist's identity, the lobbyist's client, the subject matter of the legislative representation, and the lobbyist's fees.

Although the focus of federal lobbying regulation has remained much the same—requiring public disclosure of lobbyists' finances and of the interests they represent—the 1946 Lobbying Act was less well tailored to this purpose than its modern equivalent. Some of the major problems with the 1946 Lobbying Act were that it targeted only those lobbyists whose "principal purpose" was lobbying—thereby reaching the relatively few full-time professional lobbyists—and that it applied only to lobbying directed at members of Congress, rather than including lobbying of congressional staffs and officials serving in the executive branch. Another flaw of the 1946 act was that its disclosure requirements included detailed listings of lobbying expenses but failed to provide a sense of the overall purpose of the lobbying being reported.[2]

After extensive reform hearings in Congress in the early 1990s, the 1946 Lobbying Act was replaced by the Lobbying Disclosure Act of 1995,[3] which was amended in 1998.[4] The current version of the Lobbying Act continues to be the principal source of federal statutory regulation of lobbying. The new act is broad but not all-encompassing.

For the purposes of the act, "lobbyists" are defined as individuals who are employed or retained by a client to engage in "lobbying activities" in exchange for some type of compensation.[5] But a person is not considered a lobbyist if he or she spends less than 20 percent of his or her time engaging in lobbying activities for a particular client in a six-month period. "Lobbying activities" means making "lobbying contacts" and preparing for such contacts, including "research and other background work" that is intended to be used for making lobbying contacts. "Lobbying contacts" are any oral, written, or electronic communications to a "covered" official that are made "on behalf of a client with regard to" a variety of potential legislative, executive, or administrative decisions—including "the formulation, modification, or adoption of Federal legislation (including legislative proposals)." (The act, however, lists no fewer than eighteen examples of contacts that are to be treated as "exceptions" to this definition, including direct contacts by a "church, its integrated auxiliary, or a convention or association of churches.") "Covered officials" include senior officials of the executive branch, administrative agency policymakers, as well as members of Congress, their staffs, and the staffs of congressional committees.[6]

Generally, the Lobbying Act requires "lobbying firms" (or, if they are not employed by a lobbying firm, then the individual lobbyist) to register with the clerk of the House of Representatives and the secretary of the Senate. "Lobbying firms" are entities that employ one or more persons as lobbyists "on behalf of a client other than that" entity. Organizations (e.g., corporations) that have their own in-house lobbyists file a single registration. A firm (or individual lobbyist) is exempt from registering, if a particular client does not pay at least $5,000 for the lobbying services or if an organization does not spend at least $20,000 on employees who lobby on its own behalf. Registration must take place no later than 45 days after the lobbyist is employed or retained to make a "lobbying contact" or first makes such a contact.

The registration must identify both the lobbyist and the client and describe "the general issue areas in which the registrant expects to engage in lobbying activities on behalf of the client" and "to the extent practicable, the specific issues that have (as of the date of the registration) already been addressed or are likely to be addressed in the lobbying activities." In addition, lobbyists must file semiannual reports disclosing the specific issues they have worked on, the houses of Congress or agencies contacted (but not any individuals contacted), any interests held in their lobbying activities by foreign agencies or businesses, and estimates of their lobbying fees and expenses.

The clerk of the House and the secretary of the Senate are charged with the day-to-day administration of the Lobbying Act, and they have issued administrative guidance available online at the Senate's website.[7] The U.S. attorney for the District of Columbia has the power and discretion to deal with Lobbying Act violations. The U.S. attorney may challenge alleged violations either with or without prior notice from the clerk of the House or secretary of the Senate. Punishment consists of a "civil penalty" and applies to anyone who "knowingly fails to (1) remedy a defective filing within 60 days after notice of such a defect by the Secretary of the Senate or the Clerk of the House of Representatives; or (2) comply with any other provision of [the Lobbying] Act." Those who are found responsible for such violations may face civil fines of up to $50,000.[8]

The only criminal penalties that may be imposed under the Lobbying Act are for public officials who lobby on behalf of foreign governments, organizations, or individuals.[9] This provision of the Lobbying Act applies to members of Congress and to persons acting on behalf of the United States or a federal agency. The sanctions for this type of lobbying include fines and imprisonment for up to two years, or both.

OTHER FEDERAL LAWS AND REGULATIONS THAT RESTRICT LOBBYING

A number of other federal laws are not directly aimed at lobbyists but significantly restrict lobbying techniques and activities. We review each in turn.

Bribery and Gratuity Laws and Rules

There are two subsets of bribery laws: those of broad application, aimed at all "public officials," and the gift rules specific to the Senate and the House. Both sets of rules obviously limit the degree to which lobbyists may use cash and gifts to curry favor with policymakers.

The first set prohibits any person from giving, offering, or even promising to give "anything of value" to any public official, including members of Congress and their staffs, in exchange with the "intent to influence any official act."[10] The same provision makes it a crime for the public official to take or agree to take "anything of value" for "being influenced in the performance of any official act." These are the well-settled prohibitions against bribery.

On a somewhat more subtle level, federal law also punishes giving or receiving gratuities—expressions of appreciation for a public official's actions—even if there was no prior agreement on a quid pro quo intended to motivate that action. Thus, it is a crime—albeit one punished less severely than an outright bribe—for a person to give or offer to give anything to a public official "because of any official act performed or to be performed by such public official."[11] The recipient is equally guilty if he or she accepts anything of value "because of any official act performed." The key term "anything of value" is not defined in the statute, but it covers any money or tangible gift of more than nominal intrinsic worth.

The congressional gift rules set limits on the nature and monetary value of the gifts that members, officers, and employees of the House and Senate may receive. Generally, Senate rules state that members, officers, and employees may accept only gifts valued at less than $50, where the total value of gifts from any one source is less than $100.[12] In the House, gifts are unacceptable regardless of their dollar value.[13]

There are, however, twenty-four exceptions to the House and Senate rules, which are extensive enough that some in the press have dubbed them "loopholes."[14] These exemptions allow gifts from family and friends, political contributions, entrance fees to widely attended and charity events, and gifts from governments, to name but a few. Perhaps the most controversial of these exceptions is the one that allows political contributions. This exception is made up of two separate elements: one allowing members of Congress to receive contributions for any federal, state, or local campaign and tickets to any type of political fundraising event, and the other allowing political organizations to pay for refreshments, transportation, and similar benefits in connection with a fundraising or campaign event.[15]

Although these exemptions may seem to open the door for gifts from those seeking to curry the favor of members of Congress, several rules restrict gifts from lobbyists. For example, lobbyists are prohibited from making donations that would indirectly benefit members of Congress, such as donating money to charities or conferences run by members of Congress. Moreover, lobbyists may only give gifts of "personal hospitality" to members of Congress if they are genuinely personal friends. Finally, lobbyists may not cover a member's travel expenses[16] or contribute to a member's legal expense fund.[17]

Ethics in Government Act

The Ethics in Government Act imposes extensive personal financial disclosure requirements on senior federal officials, including the president, the vice president, members of Congress, the federal judiciary, and upper-level officers and employees of the legislative and executive branches.[18] The financial disclosure reports required by the act contain detailed information about the official's income, gifts and reimbursements received, and property holdings.[19] Thus, the information is supposed to reveal financial relationships with persons who may be seeking to influence government policy. Unless filed with an intelligence organization such as the Central Intelligence Agency or National Security Agency, these disclosure reports are available to the public.[20]

Any person who knowingly or willfully falsifies or fails to file these disclosure reports may be sued by the Department of Justice. Violations of the act carry a penalty up to $5,000.[21]

The Byrd Amendment

A provision, known colloquially as the Byrd Amendment,[22] prohibits the use of federal funds to lobby for any type of a federal award (i.e., a federal contract, grant, loan, or cooperative agreement). To the same end, this provision requires the recipient of a federal award to disclose to the awarding agency certain payments made to influence the award. The law applies equally to nonprofit entities, state and local governments, and businesses and subcontractors at any level.

Internal Revenue Code

There are several Internal Revenue Code (IRC) provisions of interest to lobbyists. Essentially, the IRC provides limits on the tax deductions that businesses and trade associations may claim for their lobbying expenses. For example, the Omnibus Budget Reconciliation Act of 1993,[23] which went into effect in January 1994, repealed a previous income-tax deduction for expenses related to communication with and direct lobbying of certain executive branch officials.

In addition, the IRC places limits on lobbying by tax-exempt organizations. Specifically, tax-exempt organizations may not have lobbying comprise a "substantial part" of their activities.[24] Moreover, if a tax-exempt organization conducts activities related to matters "of direct financial interest to the donor's trade or business," a business enterprise cannot claim tax deductions for charitable contributions to that organization.[25]

Foreign Agents Registration Act

Amended in 1996, the Foreign Agents Registration Act (FARA)[26] is aimed at lobbying and political activities conducted in the United States on behalf of foreign businesses and governmental interests. Originally created to require public disclosure of Nazi propaganda efforts in the United States, FARA has evolved into a law that principally applies to individuals acting as agents of foreign governments or political parties. Technically, FARA applies to anyone who acts as an "agent of a foreign principal" in attempting to influence Congress, federal agencies, or American public opinion with respect to any U.S. political matter. These foreign principals may include foreign governments, political parties, and any persons, corporations, or associations outside the United States. To be considered an "agent" of a foreign principal under the FARA, a person must be acting on behalf of an entity whose activities are "directly or indirectly supervised, directed, controlled, financed, or subsidized in whole or in major part by a foreign principal."[27] Those parties who fall under the scope of FARA are required to register with the Department of Justice within ten days of the covered action, as well as to provide detailed supplemental filings for each six-month period thereafter.

FARA does include several exemptions, the most important for lobbyists being the one granted to persons who register under the Lobbying Act in connection with their representation of foreign clients. As a result of the Technical Amendments made to the Lobbying Act in 1998, persons serving as agents of foreign principals may register under the Lobbying Act instead of FARA, regardless of whether or not they meet the monetary and time thresholds imposed by the Lobbying Act. This exemption, however, does not apply if the lobbyist's foreign client is a foreign government or political party.[28]

Office of Management and Budget Regulation of Nonprofit Organizations' Lobbying Costs

The Office of Management and Budget has issued regulations (summed up in the circular "Cost Principles for Nonprofit Organizations"[29]) that aim to avoid the appearance that the federal government might be awarding grants and contracts to organizations advocating particular points of view. These regulations limit the extent to which lobbying costs may be reimbursed in federal government contracts, grants, and other agreements with nonprofit organizations.

Antitrust Procedures and Penalties Act (Tunney Act)

The Antitrust Procedures and Penalties Act,[30] known as the Tunney Act, was created to guarantee that settlements in antitrust actions brought by the government genuinely serve the public interest. Generally, the Tunney Act requires that courts impose an independent review of the settlement terms negotiated by the Department of Justice. The portion of the act that affects lobbyists, however, is the requirement that lobbying on behalf of defendants, of "any officer or employee of the United States concerning or relevant to [the consent decree] proposal" be disclosed.[31] This provision does, however, exclude communications between the defendant's attorney and the attorney general or employees of the Justice Department.[32]

Public Utility Holding Company Act of 1935

The Public Utility Holding Company Act of 1935[33] specifically targets registered public utility holding company employees who engage in lobbying regarding matters affecting any registered holding company or subsidiary company. Under this act, these persons are required to register, engage in extensive disclosure,[34] and file period reporting of expenses and compensation with the Securities and Exchange Commission (SEC).

ADMINSTRATIVE ENFORCEMENT OF LOBBYING STANDARDS

LEGISLATIVE BRANCH

Senate Select Committee on Ethics

The six-member Senate Select Committee on Ethics essentially oversees the self-governance of the Senate.[35] Among the committee's various powers: to receive and investigate complaints of improper conduct by members of the Senate, to report violations of any law to the appropriate federal or state authorities, and to recommend disciplinary action against members and staff. Notably for lobbyists, the committee also is responsible for regulating the receipt and disposition of gifts from foreign governments to members and for Senate implementation of the public financial disclosure requirements of the Ethics in Government Act. Moreover, the committee has the power to render advisory opinions on the application of Senate rules to members and to recommend rules needed to ensure appropriate Senate standards of conduct.

House Committee on Standards of Official Conduct

The House Committee on Standards of Official Conduct is the supervising ethics office for the House of Representatives.[36] The committee regulates House members' campaign activities, their involvement with outside entities, and their financial disclosure.

Another of the committee's duties is the issuance of the Ethics Manual for Members, Officers, and Employees of the House.[37] In addition, the committee is responsible for investigating House members' ethical violations and for issuing advisory opinions on House ethical issues.

Clerk of the House

Members, officers, and certain employees of the House and related offices, as well as candidates for the House, must file financial disclosure statements with the clerk of the House.[38] These financial disclosure reports include information about the source, type, amount, or value of the relevant persons' incomes.

The clerk is responsible for printing and distributing members' financial disclosure reports each year. In addition, the Office of the Clerk serves as the official depository of all public disclosure documents. Thus persons who wish to review these records can fill out requests and view the records at the Office of the Clerk.

EXECUTIVE BRANCH

The Office of Government Ethics (OGE) is the body charged with overseeing ethics for the executive branch. The office, originally established by the Ethics in Government Act of 1978,[39] became a separate organization under the Office of Government Ethics Reauthorization Act of 1988 on October 1, 1989.[40] The act administered by OGE restricts gifts to executive branch employees from "outside sources"—persons or organizations who may have a significant interest in having a member of the executive branch perform, or not perform, his official duties. OGE also requires certain high-level executive branch employees to file financial disclosure reports with detailed information on their assets and sources of income.[41]

U.S. Office of Special Counsel

The U.S. Office of Special Counsel has jurisdiction over all matters involving the Hatch Political Activity Act,[42] an act which prohibits federal employees from engaging in certain political activities.

REGULATION OF CAMPAIGN FINANCE

A chapter on lobbying regulation requires at least some mention of the laws governing campaign finance, a topic that has for years stirred debate in Congress, in the press, and among the public at large. Extensive discussion of these laws and of various reform proposals is, however, beyond the scope of this chapter.

PRIMARY FEDERAL CAMPAIGN FINANCE LEGISLATION

In brief, there are essentially four areas of federal campaign finance law: (1) the laws addressing the disclosure requirements and contribution limits for federal elections; (2) the regulations covering federal subsidies to presidential nominating conventions and to presidential primary and general election campaigns; (3) the criminal laws prohibiting fraudulent and coercive practices in connection with elections; and (4) the various regulations enforced by executive departments and administrative agencies other than the Federal Election Commission.

The first of these categories, the spending limits and disclosure requirements specific to federal elections, is codified primarily in the main body of the Federal Election Campaign Act (FECA), which was extensively amended in March 2002, after years of debate, by the Bipartisan Campaign Reform Act of 2002.[43] FECA—principally administered by the Federal Election Commission—limits the financial contributions that individuals,[44] political committees,[45] and political parties[46] may make to federal election campaigns. Although the act originally curbed campaign expenditures as well, these limitations have for the most part been struck down as unconstitutional.[47] In addition, the act requires political action committees, and in some cases individuals, to file reports disclosing receipts and disbursements made to influence public elections.

The laws addressing federal subsidies to presidential campaigns and nominating conventions are contained in the IRC, and, like FECA, are administered by the Federal Election Commission.[48] Basically, these provisions mandate that, if a major party candidate elects to receive federal subsidies, the candidate's campaign may not also receive private money for "qualified campaign expenses." Candidates may solicit and receive private money, however, to cover legal and accounting expenses needed to comply with campaign finance laws.

The Federal Election Commission has the power to investigate violations of either the IRC or FECA, either on its own or in response to a complaint, as long as it has reason to believe that a violation has occurred. However, the commission encourages voluntary compliance with campaign finance laws, even after a violation of these laws has been found. Moreover, the commission may only seek civil judicial relief if it is unable to formulate a conciliation agreement with the violating party.

The criminal laws relating to campaign finance are those aimed at preventing fraud and coercion in voting. They can be found in Title 18 of the U.S. Code. These laws restrict, for example, bribes made to influence voting,[49] promises of benefits or employment granted as a reward for political activity[50] or to procure a contribution to a candidate or political party,[51] and the solicitation or receipt of financial contributions within government buildings.[52] The code also prohibits the use of a federal relief appropriation for the purpose of influencing any person in the exercise of his right to vote.[53]

The fourth type of campaign finance legislation, the regulations enforced by agencies other than the Federal Election Commission, encompasses rules promulgated by organizations including the Federal Communications Commission[54] and the SEC.[55] Federal tax law also wields substantial influence on campaign finance.[56]

Finally, although these laws are not specifically targeted to campaign finance, the Hatch Political Activity Act, the Federal Lobbying Act, and the Ethics in Government Act[57] place some restrictions on campaign expenditures.

REGULATION OF POLITICAL ACTION COMMITTEES

One important mechanism in developing influence with legislative policymakers and securing access to them is the political action committee (PAC). Entities such as corporations that are barred from making direct contributions to a federal candidate's election campaign may nevertheless help raise substantial sums for the candidate's campaign by organizing a PAC.

FECA defines a political committee as a "committee, club, association or other group of persons" that either receives or spends more than $1,000 with the purpose of influencing a federal election.[58] PACs, sometimes known as "separate segregated funds," are a particular subset of political committees; they are established by corporations or by labor unions and are regulated by FECA regardless of the dollar amount of their receipts or expenses.

FECA requires PACs to include written disclaimers on all sponsored political communication, including political advertisements that either solicit money or advocate particular candidates. These disclaimers must identify who paid for the communication and clarify whether or not it was authorized by the political candidate. If it was not authorized by the candidate, the disclaimer must also identify who did authorize it.

Notably, there is some latitude granted to these political communications. First, newspapers, magazines, and other media may not charge higher rates for political communications than are charged for "comparable" uses of the same space.[59] Second, corporate communications that are sent only to a corporation's stockholders, employees, and their families are exempt from the disclaimer requirements.[60]

CONSTITUTIONAL LIMITATIONS ON LOBBYING REGULATION

Lobbying is one means of seeking to influence the policy choices made by elected officials who are expected to be responsive to the views of the citizenry. It is, therefore, a legitimate part of the democratic process. Because of the role lobbying may properly play in the political process, the U.S. Constitution imposes significant restraints on the extent to which legislation may be used to regulate lobbying. Questions about the constitutionality of lobbying regulation are often framed in terms of the First Amendment, because the legislative restrictions on lobbying potentially impinge upon three distinct First Amendment rights: the freedom of speech, the right of the people to petition their government for redress of grievances, and the implied right of associational privacy.[61]

The Supreme Court has generally upheld the constitutionality of the Federal Regulation of Lobbying Act.[62] It has also sustained the provisions in the Federal Election Campaign Act that limit or regulate direct contributions to candidates and their election campaigns.[63] In the landmark case of *Buckley v. Valeo,* the Supreme Court explained that FECA's limits on the amounts citizens may contribute directly to a candidate's campaign fund and the act's accompanying disclosure requirements were justified by the following government interests: (1) providing the public with information about candidates and the interests to which these candidates are most likely to be responsive; (2) deterring corruption and the appearance of corruption; and (3) gathering data necessary to detect violation of the contribution ceilings.[64]

Nevertheless, there have been instances in which either the Supreme Court or lower courts have found lobbying regulations to be in violation of the First Amendment. For example, Buckley and later cases have struck down limits on independent expenditures made to advance or oppose a particular candidacy.[65] The Supreme Court has viewed a person's desire to spend his or her own money to promote a particular candidacy as a form of protected political speech and expression, which government may regulate and restrict only under the most demanding standards. Lobbying legislation has been found unduly burdensome on First Amendment rights where the challenged law would be used to target particularly vulnerable groups.[66] Courts also have upheld First Amendment challenges against laws that prohibited distribution of anonymous campaign literature and laws that imposed taxes on lobbyists, on the grounds that these laws violate freedom of speech.[67]

It has been suggested that federal lobbying regulation may also be challenged as a breach of the First Amendment's establishment clause, which has been interpreted to prohibit the government from granting especially favorable treatment to religious organizations.[68] In its definition of lobbying activities, however, the Lobbying Disclosure Act exempts communications to legislative and executive branch officials by churches and other religious organizations.[69] One may argue, therefore, that this act's definition of lobbying violates the establishment clause because, in allowing religious organizations to avoid disclosure of their lobbying efforts directed at public officials, it grants especially favorable treatment to religious organizations. Religious groups have a substantial rejoinder, stressing that Congress is simply accommodating their interests protected under the First Amendment's free exercise of religion clause and that churches should be exempt from laws that substantially interfere with their religious practice. Although Congress has not yet agreed to waive the application of all laws that may burden religious practice,[70] it apparently made this accommodation in dealing specifically with lobbying.

CONCLUSION

As this brief discussion suggests, the practice of lobbying at the federal level is subject to various regulatory arrangements, which differ in focus and effects. These arrangements nevertheless provide lobbying with the breathing room required by its constitutionally protected role in our system of representative government.

NOTES

1. Federal Regulation of Lobbying Act of 1946, 60 Stat. 839 (1946), 2 U.S.C. §261–270 (1976).
2. See Section of Admin. Law and Regulatory Practice, American Bar Association, *The Lobbying Manual: A Compliance Guide for Lawyers and Lobbyists,* 2d edition, ed. William V. Luneburg (Chicago: American Bar Association, 1998), 27 [hereinafter *Lobbying Manual*]. For a comprehensive description of the 1946 Lobbying Act, generally see Thomas J. Schwarz and Alan G. Straus, *Federal Regulation of Campaign Finance and Political Activity,* vol. 1, §104, chap. 9 (New York: Matthew Bender & Co., 1985).
3. Lobbying Disclosure Act of 1995, Pub. L. No. 104-65, §2, 109 Stat. 691 (1995) (codified as 2 U.S.C.A. §§1601–12, 1997).
4. Lobbying Disclosure Technical Amendments Act of 1998, Pub. L. 105–66.
5. U.S.C.A. §1605 (1997).
6. The Lobbying Act also covers communications with officers or employees working with the Executive Office of the President, congressional commit-

tees, leadership staffs or working groups, and other officials at or above certain levels in the executive and legislative branches. See 2 U.S.C.A. §1602(3)–(4) (1997).

7. See the Senate website <www.senate.gov/contacting/contact_lobby_guidance.html>.
8. See 2 U.S.C.A. §1606(1)–(2).
9. See 18 U.S.C.A. §219(c) (Supp. 1997). This provision applies to representation of "foreign entities," defined by the same terms as "foreign principal" in the Foreign Agents Registration Act. Specifically, a "foreign entity" may be a foreign government or political party, a person outside the United States, or "a partnership, association, corporation, organization, or other combination of persons organized under the laws of or having its principal place of business in a foreign country." See 2 U.S.C.A. §1602(6), citing 22 U.S.C.A. §611(b) (defining "foreign principal").
10. U.S.C. § 201(b)(1).
11. U.S.C. § 201(c).
12. Senate Rule 35, cl. 1(b). Gifts valued at less than $10 do not count toward the $100 limit on the total value of gifts that may be received from one source. Idem.
13. House Rule 51. Note that there is an exception to this rule for "items of nominal value." Because the House committee has not defined "nominal value," however, there is no set monetary value below which gifts are acceptable.
14. Senate Rule 35, cl. 1(c)(4)(A) and 1(c)(17); House Rule 51, cl. 1(c)(16).
15. The exemption specifically allows for "attendance at a fund-raising event sponsored by a political organization described in section 527(e) of the Internal Revenue Code of 1986." The IRC definition of political organization includes political parties, campaign committees, multicandidate committees, political action committees, and other fund-raising organizations giving money to influence federal, state, or local elections.
16. Senate Rule 35, cl. 2(a)(1); House Rule 51, cl. 2(a)(1).
17. Senate Rule 35, cl. 1(c)(5) and 3(c); House Rule 51, cl. 1(c)(5) and 3(c).
18. Ethics in Government Act of 1978, Pub. L. 95-521, 92 Stat. 1824–67 (1978) (amended 1990).
19. Idem at §202.
20. Idem at §205.

21. Idem at §102(6)(C)(i).

22. U.S.C. §1352.

23. Omnibus Budget Reconciliation Act of 1993, Pub. L. No. 103-66, 107 Stat. 312 (1993).

24. See I.R.C. §501(c)(3).

25. I.R.C. §170(f)(9).

26. U.S.C. §611 et seq. (1990 and Supp. 1996).

27. U.S.C. §611(c)(i) (1990); 28 C.F.R. §5.100(a)(9) (1996).

28. U.S.C. §611(c)(1) (1990); 28 C.F.R. §5.100(a)(9) (1996); Section 8, Pub. L. 105-166 (1998).

29. Office of Management and Budget Circular A-122, "Cost Principles for Nonprofit Organizations," promulgated in 45 *Fed. Reg.* 46,022 (1980), official correction in 46 *Fed. Reg.* 17,185 (1981), amended in 49 *Fed. Reg.* 18,260 (1984), amended in 49 *Fed. Reg.* 19,588 (1984), amended in 52 *Fed. Reg.* 19,788 (1987), and amended in 60 *Fed. Reg.* 52,516 (1995).

30. U.S.C. §16(a)–(i) (1988).

31. U.S.C. §16(g) (1990).

32. U.S.C. §16(g) (1988).

33. U.S.C.A. §79 et seq.

34. The Public Utility Holding Company Lobbying Act requires disclosure to the Securities and Exchange Commission of the "subject matter in respect of which [the employee engaging in lobbying] is retained or employed," the "nature and character of such retainer or employment," and the "amount of compensation received or to be received . . . directly or indirectly, in connection [with the retainer or employment]." Idem.

35. The U.S. Constitution grants the Senate the authority to "determine the Rules of its proceedings, punish its Members for disorderly behavior, and, with the concurrence of two thirds, expel a Member." U.S. Const., art. 1, §5.

36. See 5 U.S.C. §7353.

37. Available at <www.house.gov/ethics/ethicforward.html>.

38. See Title I of the Ethics in Government Act of 1978, as amended (5 U.S.C. app. 4, §§101 et seq.)

39. Pub. L. 95-521, 92 Stat. 1824–67.

40. Pub. L. 100-598, 102 Stat. 3031.

41. Persons required to file public financial disclosure reports include the president, the vice president, administrative law judges, civilian employees in the

Executive Office of the President who hold a commission of appointment from the president, and officers or employees in the executive branch whose position is classified above GS-15 on the General Schedule prescribed by 5 U.S. 5332. For a complete listing of the persons covered by OGE, see the definition of "public filer" in 5 C.F.R. §2634.202. For a description of the contents of the public financial disclosure reports required by OGE, see 5 C.F.R. §2634.301–11.

42. Hatch Political Activity Act, ch. 410, 53 Stat. 1147 (Aug. 2, 1939).

43. Federal Election Campaign Act, 2 U.S.C. §§431–55 (1976 & Supp. III 1979); 11 C.F.R. §§100.1–146.1. The Bipartisan Campaign Reform Act of 2002, Pub. L. 107-155, 116 Stat. 81 (2002), imposes additional limits on campaign contributions made to or received by political parties, restricts corporate and labor expenditures for electioneering communications, and creates new reporting requirements, among other changes to FECA and related statutes.

44. U.S.C. §441a(a)(1), (3).

45. U.S.C. §441a(a)(1)–(2), (d), (f).

46. U.S.C. §441a(d).

47. See *Buckley v. Valeo,* 424 U.S. 1 (1976); *F.E.C. v. Nat'l Conservative Political Action Comm.,* 470 U.S. 480 (1985). But see *Nixon v. Shrink Missouri Gov't PAC,* 528 U.S. 377 402 (2000) (reasoning that statutes imposing spending limits are not automatically unconstitutional, but should be subjected to a balancing of the state's interests against the public interest if the law seeks "a fairer electoral debate through contribution limits").

48. See I.R.C. §§ 9001–13, 9031–42 (Supp. III 1979).

49. U.S.C. §597 (1976).

50. U.S.C. §600 (1976).

51. U.S.C. §601 (Supp. III 1979).

52. U.S.C. §607 (Supp. III 1979). There are some exceptions for contributions made within government buildings serving the legislative branch.

53. U.S.C. §600 (1976).

54. See 47 C.F.R. §§ 64.801–4, 73.120–23, 73.290–91, 73.590–91, 73.657–79, et seq.

55. See Release No. 34-10673 (Mar. 8, 1974), Fed. Sec. L. Rep. (CCH para. 23,509 A) (reflecting the SEC's interest in the disclosure of corporate political activities).

56. E.g., federal tax law influences the availability of tax credits for certain political contributions, the taxability of certain sources of income for political organizations, and the availability of tax benefits to organizations engaged in certain types of political activity.

57. See infra Part II.B.1.

58. C.F.R. §100.5(a).

59. C.F.R. §110.11(b)(1).

60. C.F.R. §110.11(a)(7), 114.1(j).

61. "Congress shall make no law . . . abridging the freedom of speech, or of the press; or the right of the people peaceably to assemble, and to petition the Government for a redress of grievances" (emphasis added); U.S. Const., amend. I. The right of associational privacy, though not specifically mentioned in the text of the First Amendment, is said to derive from the freedoms of speech and of assembly.

62. See *United States v. Harris,* 347 U.S. 612 (1954) (upholding the constitutionality of the Federal Regulation of Lobbying Act of 1946).

63. See *Buckley v. Valeo,* 424 U.S. 1, 96 S. Ct. 612 (1976) (upholding the Federal Election Campaign Act's disclosure obligations).

64. *Buckley,* 424 U.S. at 66–68.

65. Idem at 19, 39; *Ficker v. Montgomery Bd. of Elections,* 670 F. Supp. 618, 620–21 (1985); *Federal Election Comm'n v. Nat'l Conservative Political Action Comm.,* 105 S. Ct. 1459 (1985) (invalidating restrictions on political spending by political action committees); *Federal Election Comm'n v. Mass. Citizens for Life,* 479 U.S. 238, 259–60 (1986) (reasoning that restrictions on independent spending require compelling justification).

66. *Brown v. Socialist Workers '74 Campaign Comm. (Ohio),* 459 U.S. 87 (1982) (holding that Ohio campaign finance laws could not be used against the Socialist Workers Party because there was a reasonable possibility that the laws would be used to harass the group).

67. See *Vermont Soc'y of Ass'n Executives v. Milne, Vt.,* No. 2000-032 (June 8, 2001) (holding that a tax singling out lobbyists targeted core political speech); *McIntyre v. Ohio Elections Comm'n.,* 116 S. Ct. 1153, 1523 (1995) (holding that laws prohibiting distribution of anonymous campaign literature violated freedom of speech).

68. Letter from Andrew Fois, assistant attorney general, to the Honorable Henry Hyde, chairman, House Committee on the Judiciary (Nov. 7, 1995), contained in H.R. Rep. 104-339, at 28 (1995) (citing, inter alia, *Board of Educ. of Kiryas Joel v. Grument,* 512 U.S. 687 (1994) (plurality opinion) to the effect that the establishment clause requires that the government "pursue a course of neutrality toward religion, favoring neither one religion over others nor religious adherents collectively over-nonadherents"), cited in *Lobbying Manual,* supra note 2, at 97.

69. U.S.C. §1602(8)(B)(xviii) (2001).

70. Congress failed to ratify the proposed Religious Freedom Act of 1993, which would have allowed accommodations for religious groups where the law "substantially burden[ed] religious exercise without compelling justification." 42 U.S.C.A. §2000(b)(a)(3). This type of religious accommodation also has been rejected by U.S. courts. See *City of Boerne v. Flores,* 117 S. Ct. 2157 (1997) (overruling the Religious Freedom Act of 1993).

5 THE ETHICS OF POLITICAL ADVOCACY AND THE INTEGRITY OF THE DEMOCRATIC PROCESS

In the preceding chapters, we have identified the ethical concerns raised by the practice of lobbying, clarified the purpose and method of ethics, examined the state of the lobbying profession in the United States today, and reviewed the legal regulations that apply to lobbying the federal government. This chapter complements the ones above by exploring the ethics of political advocacy in a representative democracy, and it seeks to show how public advocacy can both support and subvert the democratic process.

U.S. law and custom recognize the right of all citizens to petition their government for redress of grievances. Political advocacy plays an important role in a representative democracy by providing essential information to elected officials and ensuring their accountability to the people at large. It is essential, however, to distinguish between the existence of political rights and their responsible exercise. The law guarantees the protection of rights; ethics seeks to determine when they are used in a legitimate and responsible manner. All rights, to be effective, must be complemented by corresponding obligations. Governments have the explicit obligation to protect the liberties and to fulfill the basic needs of their citizens. But citizens have obligations as well, obligations to one another and to the political community to which they belong. When governments violate the liberties of their citizens, or when citizens shirk their civic obligations to the commonwealth, the predictable result is public discontent and a gradual loss of faith in the political process. The irresponsible exercise of lobbying can take either of these corrupted forms: It can undermine the impartiality of public officials or it can abuse the right of petition, using it for narrow and partisan purposes that violate its historic justification.

Our ethical analysis of contemporary political advocacy draws on multiple sources. It is based on the interviews and group discussions conducted by the team, on several decades of critical scholarship that seeks to explain and assess the practice of lobbying, and on important work in normative democratic theory. It takes into account the different perspectives of insiders, those engaged in some aspect of the complex lobbying process, and outsiders, informed citizens and scholars who are deeply concerned about the health of American democracy.

CIVIC DISCONTENT

Public confidence in the integrity and effectiveness of the U.S. government is eroding. The loss of trust extends to public officials, the electoral process, and the manner in which public policy and law are shaped and implemented. The signs of democratic discontent are many: declining levels of voter participation; the indifference and disaffection of the young; the reluctance of serious citizens to enter public life; the broad appeal of political candidates calling for systemic reform (e.g., U.S. senator John McCain, former senator Bill Bradley, and Ralph Nader); high levels of apathy, distrust, and even contempt for the state of American politics.[1]

What accounts for this pattern of civic withdrawal and disaffection? There are many contributing factors, but the general explanation is clear. When the people do not believe that the political process is just and effective, they are reluctant to participate in it. Popular perceptions of political unfairness are quite specific. They include the role of money in financing political campaigns, the grave inequalities of access and influence that money buys, the disproportionate power of organized interests on democratic decision making, the disturbing impotence of the national government in addressing vital public concerns, and profound inequalities in economic and political power among U.S. citizens.

The pervasive belief that government serves the interests of the powerful has demoralized American democracy. It has weakened support for government, generated distrust of public officials, and significantly reduced the civic engagement of ordinary citizens.

As public participation in politics has declined, the power and influence of lobbyists have increased. In fact, lobbying, the deliberate attempt to influence political decisions through various forms of public advocacy, has become a critical factor in both the electoral and governing process. Numerous attempts have been made to describe and explain how lobbying actually works. Our ethical appraisal of American lobbying draws on both practical experience and empirical scholarship while addressing specifically normative questions: (1) What moral principles and precepts govern the practice of lobbyists? (2) What does lobbying contribute to the conduct of democratic government? What genuine goods does it achieve? What constitutional rights does it protect? (3) What are its moral and political limitations? How does lobbying affect the common good and the needs of the poor and the powerless? And of greatest importance, perhaps: How does lobbying affect the health of American democracy—the integrity of the decision-making process, the accountability of public officials, the confidence of the people in their government, and the responsible engagement of ordinary citizens in public affairs?

HISTORICAL CONTEXT

During the past seventy years, the power and influence of the federal government have steadily increased. The New Deal and the Great Society helped to create a limited welfare state. The Cold War transformed the United States into a global superpower. The regulatory activity of federal agencies extended the influence of government into every sector of the economy and society. The decisions made by public officials in Washington regularly affect business, labor, education, the environment, and public health—the list of affected parties nearly coincides with the organized interests seeking to influence the conduct of government.

A continental democracy like the United States needs the mediating institutions of civil society to connect its citizens with their government and to protect them against abuses of public power. For several reasons, American civil society has weakened during the past thirty years. Loyalty to political parties is down; the press has become less responsible; the mainstream churches and the academy have lost moral authority. As these traditional institutions have grown weaker, lobbyists, lawyers, organized interest groups, and skilled professional advocates have expanded in number and influence. But not only their numbers have grown. They have become highly skilled and effective in shaping legislation, advancing or opposing public agendas, influencing political appointments, and affecting the implementation of public policy and law.

Special interest lobbying has moved far beyond the purchase of political access and influence. As the struggle over health care reform revealed, organized interests now use all the tools of modern political communications to advance their objectives: massive and expensive grassroots lobbying, shaping public opinion through media campaigns and political advertising, fund-raising for candidates who are increasingly dependent on organized interests for electoral support, targeting key members of congressional committees, and so on. The cost, size, power, and reach of these opinion- and decision-shaping effects are unprecedented.

The incessant scramble for money both propels and paralyzes political life. It preoccupies public officials and their staffs, heightens their dependence on organized interests, drives conscientious citizens out of electoral politics, and deepens the distrust of ordinary citizens for their elected representatives.

How has the national balance of political power shifted? The federal government has grown stronger, but civil society is weaker. Organized interests have gained greater political influence, but the traditional parties are in decline. Lobbyists and partisan advocates basically drive the public agenda, while ordinary citizens worry that their opinions and concerns will not be heard or heeded.

THE RIGHT OF PETITION

The First Amendment to the Constitution guarantees the American people the right to petition the government for a redress of grievances. U.S. law and custom also support the right of voluntary association—the freedom of citizens to join together in support of shared principles, opinions, and interests. The creation of interest groups, therefore, and the practice of political lobbying are traditional rights of U.S. citizens. Like other civic rights, they provide a necessary check on governmental power and enable aggrieved citizens or groups to seek redress for public or private injury.

Lobbying can also serve a valuable educational function. Honest and well-informed lobbyists provide members of Congress and their staffs, the communications media, and the American public with relevant information and incisive arguments bearing on matters of public debate. Voluntary associations of citizens united in a common cause are also a significant source of political power. They can act in their own right, for good or ill, but they can also exert significant influence on public policy and law and on the vitality of civic life.

THE POWER OF ORGANIZED INTERESTS

In a democratic society, voluntary associations of all kinds are strongly encouraged. These include associations of principle like the League of Women Voters; associations of shared moral passion, like the pro-life and pro-choice groups; charitable associations like the Red Cross and Oxfam; popular coalitions for political and social reform like the civil rights and environmental movements; political parties of quite different civic persuasions; and associations of shared economic interest like the National Association of Manufacturers and the AFL-CIO.

What political resources do these voluntary associations possess? They have money, organizational ability, relevant knowledge and information, energetic and active members, the allegiance of voters, and a reputation for significant political clout. Economic resources, though they are only one source of public power, have a substantial influence on American politics. They not only fund the campaigns of political candidates, but they can be used to hire skilled professionals, lawyers, lobbyists, public relations strategists, and media experts, to advance the economic interests of well-financed clients. "Deep pockets speak," according to experienced observers and participants, because unequal economic power translates into disproportionate political influence on both the electoral and governing processes.

The well-documented interdependence of economic and political power is a principal source of democratic discontent. It creates a systemic inequality in the access of citizens to public officials and in the shaping of public policy. Organized interests with substantial political power directly affect the normal operations of government. They frame the national policy agenda; prevent unwanted reform; advance or oppose political appointments; influence legislative and regulatory decisions; and, through strategic media campaigns, effectively shape public opinion on controversial national issues.

THE PRACTICE OF LOBBYING: INTERNAL NORMS AND RESPONSIBILITIES

The constitutional right to petition the government is guaranteed by U.S. law and custom. But the existence of this right does not ensure its responsible exercise. Lobbyists have moral and civic obligations as well as rights, and they are accountable for their conduct to several different groups of citizens. They have professional responsibilities to the clients who hire them, to the elected officials and their staffs whom they actively lobby, and to the public media whose coverage of political affairs they seek to influence. They also have civic obligations to their country, for the hired lobbyist is also an engaged citizen with a citizen's duty to promote the public good.

The universal norms that govern all human action also apply to the conduct of lobbyists. These include prescriptive norms like telling the truth, promoting justice, and treating other persons with integrity and respect. They also include the proscriptive norms that forbid bribery, distortion, flattery, and fraud. Several of the relevant norms arise from the distinctive practices in which lobbyists engage. These profession specific norms include (1) compliance with both the letter and the spirit of existing law; (2) the avoidance of conflicts of interest; (3) the appropriate respect for confidentiality; (4) full disclosure of clients and funding sources; (5) honest and dedicated service to clients; (6) the avoidance of unjust lobbying techniques (e.g., ad hominem attacks, half-truths, scare tactics, and the artificial creation of grass roots); (7) preserving the reputation and integrity of their profession; (8) striking the appropriate balance between private interests and the common good; and (9) creating a public culture in which responsible advocacy, rather than success at any price, becomes the operative norm of practical conduct.

DEMOCRATIC LEGITIMACY

Law cannot guarantee the commitment and allegiance of democratic citizens to their country. Public trust in government and in the democratic process rests on perceived legitimacy; legitimacy, in turn, depends on the faithful observance of basic democratic precepts. The principal task of democracy is to engage its citizens and their elected representatives in discovering and promoting the public good. This formidable political project requires knowledgeable citizens with a firm commitment to the nation's well-being. Economic prosperity and peace do not guarantee that our underlying civic culture is sound and that the civic allegiance of our citizens is strong.

What are the legitimating principles on which an authentic representative democracy rests? Seven of the most important principles are worthy of note. The first principle is the political equality of all citizens. Political equality concretely means equal civic rights and obligations, reasonable access to public officials, and a significant opportunity to influence public decisions. When citizens are not political equals, when some citizens or groups enjoy greater rights or greater access and influence than others, then the moral foundations of democracy are subverted.[2]

The second principle is a reasonable process of selecting political representatives, delegating public responsibilities, and communicating public views to elected officials. Government officers are accountable to the community of citizens through free, frequent, and fair elections.

The third principle is the informed consent of the governed. Informed consent requires transparency in the decision-making process and governmental responsiveness to public needs and concerns. The fourth principle is the guaranteed protection of individual rights, including the right of all citizens to meaningful participation in the conduct of public affairs.

The fifth principle is the promotion of justice, both distributive and rectificatory. The benefits and burdens of civic cooperation should be equitably shared; both criminal punishment and civil penalties should be proportionate to the wrongdoer's offense.

The sixth principle is the long-term sustainability of the democratic community. This means giving permanent, comprehensive public goods consistent precedence over transient and parochial private interests. Because public service is a public trust, judges, legislators, and members of the executive branch are directly responsible for preserving and promoting the commonweal.

The seventh principle is that the deliberative practices of democracy should refine, enlarge, and deepen public opinion and enhance the readiness of citizens to make informed and responsible political decisions. An ethical appraisal of lobbying in the United States must carefully examine whether our existing forms of political advocacy and policy formation satisfy these requirements of democratic legitimacy.

DEEP ETHICAL CONCERNS

The practice of lobbying raises two distinct types of ethical concerns.[3] Internal concerns arise for people directly engaged in the lobbying process—whether they are clients or lobbyists, or the elected officials, their staffs, and the shapers of public opinion whom the lobbyists seek to influence. The systemic concerns arise from a growing unease about the American way of conducting public affairs.

INTERNAL CONCERNS

The most pressing internal concern is the dominant role of money in financing electoral politics and in influencing public policy. Significant inequalities in economic resources typically lead to political inequalities in representation, access, and influence. The disproportionate resources available to the wealthy and the powerful compromise the democratic principle of political equality.

Another important concern is the revolving door among government, business corporations, organized interest groups, and professional lobbyists. These rapid transitions blur the important distinction between public service and self-interested activity, and they create the impression that Washington is dominated by a narrow, self-perpetuating governing elite.

Another concern is the miseducation of the public through the irresponsible use of the media. Unethical techniques—such as distortion of issues or reliance on smear tactics and half-truths—that are ineffective in lobbying elected officials and their staffs may be quite persuasive in shaping public perceptions and fears. Lack of transparency and full disclosure in political advertising tends to conceal whom the lobbyists really represent and whose particular interests they serve. All these concerns highlight the central ethical challenge that lobbyists face: the need to balance their professional obligations to clients with their concurrent responsibility as citizens to promote justice and the common good.

SYSTEMIC CONCERNS ABOUT THE AMERICAN PRACTICE OF LOBBYING

The first systemic concern is that lobbying fosters a claimant politics based on the pursuit of self-interest and group advantage rather than a civic politics based on the discovery and enactment of the comprehensive public good. In a claimant politics, the body politic is fragmented into competing interest groups with a subsequent loss of civic solidarity and public spirit. Under these divisive conditions, the government becomes ineffective in addressing long-term national problems (e.g., entitlement reform, an equitable tax structure, economic and political inequality, protection of the environment, and the decline of the inner cities).

Well-financed lobbyists serving powerful organized interests weaken public trust in government and discourage ordinary citizens from participating in public life. Civic alienation has several causes: the raising and spending of special interest money has become a dominant form of political activity; public opinion is skillfully and cynically manipulated through political advertising and public relations; inequities of access and influence favor unfair policy decisions; and the legitimate needs of the poor, the weak, and the unorganized tend to remain unmet. The general complaint is that professional lobbying as currently practiced in the United States undermines political equality, the moral foundation of democracy.

Finally, there is the unresolved but critical tension between the economic values of free-market capitalism (competition, profit, and efficiency) and the political requirements of democratic legitimacy (equality, liberty, and justice for all).

Is the moral vision that inspired American democracy, the vision of a government of, by, and for the people, ultimately consistent with the spirit of interest-driven politics fostered by capitalism? Economic and political agents motivated by self-interest alone have minimal incentive to take the rights and concerns of others and the needs of the national community into account.

APPROPRIATE AND EFFECTIVE REFORMS

What can be done to remedy the abuses of political advocacy and the systematic inequities created by powerful organized interests?[4] What can be done to restore public confidence in the integrity and legitimacy of American democracy? It is the central thesis of this chapter that the two questions are interconnected and must be examined together. To paraphrase James Madison, we are seeking democratic remedies for democratic ills. While ensuring the traditional rights of association and public advocacy, what can be done to promote their more responsible exercise?

We need to distinguish different levels of political reform. The first is *personal* reform: Individual clients, lobbyists, public officials, journalists, and ordinary citizens can change the way they think, speak, and act in the political realm. They can more faithfully comply with the internal norms that govern their public roles, and they can more effectively balance their professional obligations and civic responsibilities. They can lead by example, by speaking and acting in ways that restore dignity and honor to political life.

The second level is *institutional and structural* reform: "Until the problem of money is dealt with, it is unrealistic to expect the political process to improve."[5] We must reform the way in which political campaigns are financed. The pay-to-play system creates major inequities in access, influence, and power. It discourages promising candidates from seeking public office, demoralizes ordinary citizens, drives them to the political sidelines, and systematically disadvantages the poor and powerless. Public confidence in government will not be restored until the pursuit and exchange of money cease to dominate American politics.

The institutions of civil society, particularly the political parties, need to be strengthened. When intermediate institutions are accessible, independent, and politically active, they connect ordinary citizens with their government and provide them with opportunities for meaningful civic education and participation.

The political media have become increasingly sensationalistic and profit driven. Their coverage of public affairs is typically superficial and slanted toward controversy. The media have largely abandoned their historic role of refining and enlarging public opinion by explaining, interpreting, and assessing policy differences and placing them in a broader, more historical frame of reference. A free and responsible press is essential to a healthy democracy and a well-informed citizenry.

All established institutions—including business firms, trade associations, and religious communities—whose conduct significantly affects the political community are subject to public norms and appraisal. Public accountability applies to everyone involved in the policymaking process, not only to elected officials. To ensure such accountability, full public disclosure of lobbyists, their clients, and their specific political initiatives and activities should be required.

The accountability of public officials to the people they represent is procedurally guaranteed by free, fair, and frequent elections. We also need to create new and credible public forums where citizens and their representatives can assemble to exchange political opinions and to deliberate together about the public good. Ordinary citizens will not return in significant numbers to the public realm until they believe their political opinions and concerns are given legitimate weight in the creation of policy and law.

The third level of reform is *cultural and intellectual*. Americans, at all levels, need to reexamine the way we think, speak, and feel about government and citizenship. We have created a political culture that emphasizes individual rights and diminishes public responsibilities, that celebrates the pursuit of self-interest and questions the possibility of civic virtues, that highlights individual misconduct and glosses over systematic unfairness, and that cultivates skeptical attitudes about disinterested citizenship and devotion to the common good.

In the original republican vision, politics, the symbol of the commonweal, enjoyed directive authority over economics, the symbol of self-interested activity. Today, politics is heavily dominated by economic interests and institutional models. The conduct of government increasingly resembles that of commercial enterprises, as marketing, bargaining, public relations, and partisan advocacy have become pervasive. Nearly everyone conceives of political action as a way of advancing limited private and group concerns.

As long as this market-driven mentality prevails and excludes other ways of conceiving political life, a sustained cultural critique of American democracy will be difficult to mount. If the pursuit of self-interest is the operative political norm, then clients, lobbyists, public officials, journalists, and citizens are fully justified in pursuing their own desires and demands, without due regard for the needs of the disadvantaged and their fiduciary obligations to posterity.

It is very important to distinguish between explicit corruption and systematic unfairness. Examples of corruption include bribery, quid pro quo contributions, lying and distortion, conflicts of interest, and violations of lobbying and campaign finance law. To check explicit corruption, we need clear rules of conduct for clients, lobbyists, and public officials and strict enforcement of them. Examples of systematic unfairness include the disproportionate influence of powerful interests, lack of adequate and fair representation for all citizens, and the absence of meaningful political equality. Institutional and cultural reform, and far more effective civic education about the requirements of a sustainable democracy, are needed to correct structural inequities and cultural prejudices.

Unfortunately, the media and the general public are more attentive to personal wrongdoing than to institutional and cultural bias. We need only consider the media coverage given to President Clinton's real or alleged misconduct as opposed to the structural problems of economic and political inequality, the role of money in driving electoral politics, the weakening of political parties, the coverage of foreign affairs, and the devolution of governmental power.

In seeking to reform American lobbying, there is a great need for sobriety and realism. There are no perfect solutions to these serious and recurrent national problems. A high level of practical wisdom is required here because good intentions are an inadequate basis for effective reform, and the law of unintended consequences remains in force. In pursuing political justice, there is a constant need to balance the claims of equality and liberty. Moreover, there are inherent limits to the corrective power of rules and regulations. All rules need to be interpreted and applied, and this discretionary, interpretive practice can follow the letter, while violating the spirit, of the law. Fundamental shifts of political attitude and outlook, both personal and cultural, are in the end even more important than codified rules. Even the most prudent institutional reforms will have limited practical effect without a deep cultural rethinking of citizenship, public service, and civic responsibility.

WHAT IS AT STAKE?

Democracy should be the most educational form of government. It should engage democratic citizens and their elected representatives in a continuous public debate about national and global well-being. American democracy today is seriously failing in its educational mission because its political leaders are losing the trust and support of ordinary citizens. Large numbers of citizens, particularly the young and disaffected, no longer believe in the legitimacy of their government and in the fairness of the democratic process.

This decline in public confidence coincides with a devalued sense of civic obligation, as citizens neglect to vote, remain uninformed and apathetic about public affairs, and surrender to the illusion of political impotence. There are deep structural reasons for this civic decline, but the growth of lobbying and the money culture that surrounds it are among the most important. Unless this serious decline is arrested and reversed, the alienation of the American people from their democracy may reach crisis proportions. The gravest ethical issue facing our country today is not the conduct of lobbyists but the state of American democracy.

NOTES

1. Civic discontent, of course, ranges across a broad spectrum. It tends to be less pronounced in those directly engaged in politics and more intense in those who have effectively withdrawn from active citizenship. In the dominant middle are the majority of citizens who support the democratic process but who experience unease about its fairness and efficacy. In this chapter, we are trying to articulate the nature and spirit of that unease.
2. Robert Dahl, *Democracy* (New Haven, Conn.: Yale University Press, 1989), 178.
3. The ethical concerns enumerated in this section reflect the different levels and sources of unease within the American electorate. Some are concerns directly voiced by lobbyists and public officials themselves, others reflect the critical perceptions of scholars and journalists, and still others the feelings and judgments of ordinary citizens. In calling them concerns, we are not endorsing their validity as evaluative judgments but pointing to sensitive areas that require public attention and scrutiny. Because we are trying to convey both the substance and tone of these civic concerns, the language employed is not meant to be morally neutral.
4. The specific principles and precepts that should govern the conduct of lobbying are articulated in chapter 7 as the Woodstock Principles. The purpose of this section is to identify the different levels of political reform to which

those principles apply. The Woodstock Principles speak directly to clients, lobbyists, and public officials; the reforms outlined here are intended to promote and restore legitimacy in every sector of American politics.

5. Elizabeth Drew, *Politics and Money: The New Road to Corruption* (New York: Macmillan, 1983), 4.

6 ETHICS IN LOBBYING: A HYPOTHETICAL CASE STUDY

This case study was created as a hypothetical situation to stimulate and guide group discussions. The goal of the overall project is to identify and articulate an appropriate and relevant set of ethical principles to guide the lobbying process. A crucial method used was to engage actual participants in the lobbying process in discussion of the kinds of issues that arise in the "real world," and the decisions and actions they consider sound in resolving those issues.

The case study seeks to illustrate the various stages in the lobbying relationship and the lobbying process at which the lobbyist may confront ethical choices. Though not every lobbying assignment involves such a wide array of potentially difficult choices, the design of the case study provides a concise, provocative, and practical illustration of key decision points and seeks to do so in a way that suggests the subtlety and complexity of many of the issues.

The focus of the inquiry is on the decisions the lobbyist must make throughout the process. The first decision, of course, is whether to accept an assignment. This question turns on the answer to several other inquiries: Do I want to work for this client? Do I want to advance the client's position? Would accepting the assignment conflict with my other personal or professional obligations?

One fundamental and often overlooked aspect of this initial inquiry emerged: To what extent may—or must—a lobbyist make a judgment about whether a client's objective is inconsistent with some notion of the broader public interest? In its starkest terms, the answer to this question rests on two alternative visions of the role of the lobbyist: either a zealous tactician bound above all to accomplish a client's goals by any means allowed by law, or a professional advocate constrained by personal civic responsibility. The choice between these opposing conceptions also influences the degree to which the lobbyist has a responsibility to try to counsel a client about whether the proposed objective is appropriate, even if the lobbyist believes it can be achieved.

The case study frames these questions of ends and means by illustrating the multifaceted relationships that are at stake among all the participants in the lobbying process: clients, lobbyists, policymakers, the news media, and the public. In essence, it stimulates reflection on what each of these interested parties may legitimately expect from the other participants. Discussion of these questions and reflection on that discussion are contained in the Woodstock Principles in chapter 7. The case study follows.

CENTRAL PARTICIPANTS

The Atkins Chemical Company is a multinational conglomerate with interests in phosphates and petrochemicals. It has both U.S. and foreign manufacturing facilities. Its headquarters is in Ohio, and it has U.S. facilities in seven states. Its chairman is Ben Butler. Butler has been a generous contributor to both major political parties. In 1988 he pleaded guilty to violating the federal election laws by making an excessive contribution to the Senate reelection campaign of Democratic Senator Clyde Chambers of Kentucky, where Atkins Chemical has a large facility. Butler is also vice chairman of the Republican Patriots, a national organization of business leaders who contribute at least $100,000 annually to the national Republican Party.

Policy Advocates, Incorporated, is a Washington-based consulting firm that specializes in legislative lobbying. It has five "directors" and twenty-five staff members. Two of the five directors are former members of Congress, one a former Senate Republican, the other a former senior Democratic member of the House. Chairing the firm is Ted Dreyfus, a lawyer who worked as a senior domestic adviser to a Republican president. Each of the directors is active in raising funds for the congressional campaign committee of one party or the other.

The Christian Alliance is a powerful collection of fundamentalist religious organizations that actively promotes its views on matters of public policy and supports or opposes national candidates based on the alliance's evaluation of their positions on the issues to which they assign a high priority.

BUSINESS BACKGROUND AND PROBLEMS

Atkins Chemical is embroiled in several high-profile disputes. Human rights groups have charged that it acquired vast phosphate holdings in Borneo by bribing the minister of natural resources and collaborating with the Indonesian army to drive subsistence farmers from the land. In ensuing disturbances, at least thirty-five natives were killed. In addition, the human rights groups allege that the miners whom Atkins Chemical employs at its Borneo site are paid only the equivalent of 20 cents an hour, work in stifling and unsanitary conditions, and are exposed to dangerous levels of carcinogens. In addition, workers trying to organize a trade union at the mine have been beaten, although there is no clear evidence who is responsible for the attacks. The region is rife with religious and ethnic tensions. All the senior managers and supervisors at the facility are Javanese Muslims; it is said that workers from the local Christian minority are confined to the most dangerous and lowest paid jobs and are excluded from any opportunity to supervise the strategically favored Muslims.

The Indonesian government denies all of these allegations, saying they are merely the result of separatist propaganda. The government also insists that these are purely internal matters. For its part, Atkins Chemical says that it is fully complying with all applicable local laws and customs.

Atkins Chemical has also been cited by the U.S. Environmental Protection Agency for discharging pollutants from its Kentucky facility into an adjoining river. A local "clean water" group contends that the pollutants have seeped into the groundwater from which surrounding farmers draw water for their crops and livestock. A prominent "plaintiffs' lawyer" is threatening to bring a class action suit on behalf of the farmers seeking millions of dollars in compensatory and punitive damages as well as an order to install costly wastewater disposal filters at Atkins Chemical's plant. The company denies responsibility for tainting the groundwater from which and has issued a press release declaring that, if forced to make further capital expenditures on nonproductive pollution control devices, the plant will become unprofitable and will be closed. Instead, production will be moved offshore. With 860 employees, the Atkins Chemical plant is the largest employer in the economically depressed county. Under current federal law, extensive benefits must be paid when a company closes a plant.

The clean water group has what it claims is a scientific report supporting its charge that Atkins Chemical's plant is the source of the pollution. The plaintiffs' lawyer also claims to have a study linking a "cluster" of liver cancers in the area to runoff from the plant.

LOBBYING PROJECT

Atkins Chemical's chairman, Ben Butler, has heard that Senator Chambers, a leading member of the liberal bloc in Congress, is planning to introduce a bill to impose a 50 percent tariff on goods imported from any country in which the secretary of state finds that workers are subjected to "gross abuse of fundamental human rights" and so informs the secretary of the treasury. The details of the bill have not yet been worked out, but reports are circulating that Senator

Chambers may be considering including several examples of such conditions, including widespread forced relocation of indigenous populations; use of military forces to repress peaceful potential protest; systematic discrimination on grounds of race, religion, or ethnicity; and disregard for prevailing standards promulgated by the International Labor Organization. Because of the possibility of covering religious discrimination, the Christian Alliance is urging key members of the Republican majority in the Senate to support the Chambers bill, if he introduces it.

Atkins Chemical has occasionally used Policy Advocates on some corporate tax issues. Butler arranged an appointment with Policy Advocate's senior director, Ted Dreyfus, and tells him he wants the firm's help on two legislative projects. First, he wants to protect his company's operation in Borneo from the kind of tariffs threatened by Senator Chambers's potential legislation. Second, he wants to initiate a legislative strategy that will either take the pressure off the Kentucky plant or provide some kind of "cover" if he decides to shut it down.

Dreyfus knows that Senator Chambers is in another difficult reelection battle, and one of his colleagues at the firm has offered to chair the senator's campaign finance committee. In addition, the firm's own former Republican senator was active in tort reform issues in the South and knows that the chairman of the relevant Senate committee is looking for a chance to argue that American business enterprise needs to be protected against money-grubbing plaintiffs' lawyers who use "junk science" to extort huge settlements for exaggerated or fictitious claims.

Policy Advocates for many years has represented several of the universities operated by the Central Baptist Convention, one of the principal members of the Christian Alliance. Dreyfus also knows that companies that have manufactured PCBs, dioxins, asbestos, and tobacco products are looking for legislation to reduce their litigation exposure. Dreyfus also knows of companies that exploit their foreign workers shamelessly and would be affected by Senator Chambers's bill.

ROLE OF THE CHRISTIAN ALLIANCE

A fieldworker for one of the largest members of the Christian Alliance has spent several years in Borneo. He has observed that the workers at Atkins Chemical's mines there seem to have better living conditions than most of the indigenous population. In addition, he knows several supervisors at the facility who are Christian and they have commended the local leadership of the company for resisting pressure from Islamic fundamentalists. The fieldworker's report reached the Washington office of the Christian Alliance. The director of legislative relations for the alliance has heard from another lobbyist that Senator Chambers, who campaigned on a "family values" plank, is having an "inappropriate relationship" with a member of his staff (although the gender of the aide was not mentioned). Chambers is scheduled to be the keynote speaker at the Christian Alliance's annual convention.

USE OF THE CASE STUDY

The ethical issues involved should be discussed from the respective points of view of (1) Atkins Chemicals, the lobbying client; (2) Policy Associates, the lobbying firm; (3) the Christian Alliance, another lobbying group; (4) Senator Chambers, the public policy decision maker; and (5) all citizens concerned about domestic and international justice.

CASE STUDY ISSUES AND QUESTIONS

GENERAL FOCUSING QUESTIONS

The fictional case study deliberately creates multiple conflicts of interest. The legitimate expectations of Atkins Chemical, Policy Associates, Senator Chambers, and the people of Indonesia and Kentucky cannot jointly be satisfied. What ethical questions and principles should guide us in addressing and resolving these conflicts?

Questions for the Executives of Atkins Chemical

1. What are the legal and moral obligations of Atkins Chemical to
    a. the indigenous Indonesian people whose land has been appropriated,
    b. the foreign workers in their Indonesian plant,
    c. the economic and environmental health of the countries and regions where their business operations are conducted,
    d. their workers in Kentucky, and
    e. their shareholders?

2. Who has regulatory jurisdiction over multinational corporations? Who has the authority to discipline them when they violate the rights of foreign workers, or severely damage the economic and environmental well-being of foreign countries?

3. How should the legal and moral obligations of Atkins Chemical constrain its business practices, both nationally and internationally? Must the pursuit of profit and competitive advantage be subordinated to the obligation to respect human rights and to safeguard the well-being of workers and citizens?

4. How do we objectively resolve ethical dilemmas of this kind? To what resources can we turn for wise and fair guidance? How should Atkins behave if it is genuinely unclear about the scope and priority of its moral obligations?

Questions for Policy Advocates

1. How should the answers to questions 1–4 above affect the practical decisions of Policy Advocates? Should they refuse to accept Atkins as a client if they believe it has failed to meet its legal and moral obligations in Indonesia and Kentucky?

2. What are the legal and moral obligations of Policy Advocates to
    a. its prospective clients,
    b. its employees and shareholders, and
    c. the people and workers of Indonesia and Kentucky?

Questions for Senator Chambers

1. How should Senator Chambers prioritize his political and moral obligations with regard to
    a. the people of Kentucky,
    b. the international human rights community,
    c. the owners and workers of Atkins Chemical, and
    d. his understandable desire for reelection?

2. Should he refuse to accept money from Atkins Chemical in his reelection campaign?

3. Should he soften his support for foreign workers' rights to protect the jobs of Atkins's employees in his home state?

4. How should he weigh the competing goods of a safe and sustainable environment versus the economic survival of a depressed region?

Questions for All Concerned Citizens

1. How should we respond as citizens if there is no way to resolve these interdependent conflicts within the framework of existing law and in the absence of an effective moral and political consensus on multinational business practices?

2. Do our political obligations as citizens outweigh our economic obligations to the clients and companies for which we work?

SPECIFIC ISSUES AND QUESTIONS

1. What considerations should affect the decision by Policy Advocates whether to accept
     a. the client and
     b. the assignment?

2. What consultations should Dreyfus have with his colleagues within Policy Advocates before resolving these questions?

3. What should Dreyfus discuss with Atkins Chemical's Butler about
     a. the appropriateness of Atkins's goals and
     b. the arguments to be made in pursuing them?

4. What should Dreyfus discuss with Butler about changes in the business practices of Atkins Chemical?

5. To what extent, if at all, is it pertinent that the allegations against Atkins Chemical are true?

6. May Policy Advocates simply rely on the denials of misconduct
     a. by the Indonesian Government or
     b. by Atkins Chemical's plant manager, if the firm believes the allegations are true, but open to reasonable debate?

7. To what extent should or must Policy Advocates make further inquiries to find out the "real" facts about the situations in Borneo or Kentucky?

8. If Policy Advocates is aware of a confidential report done by Atkins Chemical's environmental health department tending to confirm some but not all of the allegations about the source of the Kentucky pollution and its effects, may or must the firm disclose this report in dealing with people in Congress?

9. If Policy Advocates concludes that the policy issues Atkins Chemical wants to pursue are generally sound, even if the company is individually "in the wrong," may the firm disregard its client's specific facts and make the general policy arguments without inhibition?

10. If a member of Congress or legislative aide asks Dreyfus or someone else from Policy Advocates "what is really going on," what should their answer be?

11. Does it violate the protocol of the lobbying relationship between client and lobbyist even to ask this kind of question?

12. If there is no group affirmatively advancing the cause of Senator Chambers's "human rights" legislation, to what extent does Policy Advocates have an obligation to describe the arguments in its favor?

13. Does it make a difference if the active, outside proponents of the legislative proposal consist simply of two young volunteers with a small Asian-Pacific human rights group?

14. If any liability-reform legislation needs the support of a key Democratic member of the House from Oregon, where Atkins Chemical has no facilities, may Policy Advocates suggest that the company invite him to give a 10-minute breakfast talk at a meeting of the company's "executive council" and present him with a $5,000 check—for his reelection campaign committee?

15. Suppose a member of Congress from Maine asks how he should balance the interests of destitute natives and workers on Borneo with the interests of Atkins Chemical's employee pension plan, which is heavily invested in the company's stock?

16. If a friendly member of the House Judiciary Committee is willing to offer a legislative ban on punitive damages in Clean Water Act issues and to do so at a committee mark-up without hearings or prior public notice, may Policy Advocates responsibly pursue that course?

17. If Policy Advocates has influential relationships with both the chairman and ranking minority members of the relevant Judiciary Committee subcommittee, may the firm suggest that they only allow testimony against the tort reform amendment by a single witness who is known to be inarticulate and ineffectual?

18. If Policy Advocates would not have undertaken to represent tobacco companies directly in pursuing protection against civil liability for causing injury to public health, may the firm (a) enlist their support in pursuing legislation helpful to Atkins Chemical and (b) join a coalition with them?

19. Because tobacco interests in Kentucky are a potent political force, may Policy Advocates trade support for the tobacco industry's antiliability agenda for their help in dissuading Senator Chambers from pushing his human rights tariff bill?

20. If Policy Advocates organizes Citizens to Protect American Jobs, funded entirely by Atkins Chemical, and places advertisements in key congressional districts urging voters to pressure their members of Congress to support legislation to "keep money grubbing lawyers from taking away your jobs," what must it then disclose about the real parties financing these ads and about the countervailing arguments?

21. If Dreyfus has a close friend who is a former U.S. ambassador now teaching political science at a university, may he commission him to publish an "op-ed" piece under the ambassador's own byline, arguing that principles of free trade should keep Congress from trying to dictate internal economic and social conditions in other countries?

22. Does it make a difference if Atkins Chemical pays the ambassador a stipend for his "time" in preparing the article?

23. If the policies Atkins desired are accomplished but Policy Associates actually has taken no advocacy action on this issue:

      a. What are their disclosure responsibilities?

      b. Should they still collect a fee?

7 THE WOODSTOCK PRINCIPLES FOR THE ETHICAL CONDUCT OF LOBBYING

INTRODUCTION AND DEFINITIONS

PURPOSE

These principles are intended to provide practical guidance to persons who engage in the process of lobbying. They reflect the essential considerations that a participant in this process should address and evaluate in order to perform the functions of a lobbyist with professional competence, personal integrity, and civic responsibility. The principles also address the decisions to be made by persons who retain lobbyists as well as by the persons whom the lobbyists seek to influence, so that lobbyists have a clear understanding of what is properly expected of them in their work as political agents.

Many of the principles deal with the actual practice of lobbying. Others pertain to the contexts in which lobbying occurs and the consequences of lobbying for American democracy. These principles rest on the belief that it is important for the lobbyist to remain ever mindful of an overarching issue: Does the present system of distributing and exercising political power in the United States satisfy the norms of justice and promote the general well-being of our democratic society?

Although we are acutely aware of the problem of money in American politics and of the role that fund-raising, campaign contributions, and unregulated political expenditures play in securing access to and influence with public officials, we do not directly address this critical issue in these Woodstock Principles. However, many of the principles articulated here may be relevant to the ongoing debate about money, because they address underlying concerns about the practice of lobbying today. Specific proposals to reform the financing of political campaigns have recently been voted into law. Our goal is to complement these important efforts at political reform with a set of principles that can guide other significant aspects of the lobbyist's activity.

Definition of Lobbying[1]

For the purposes of these principles, "lobbying" means the deliberate attempt to influence political decisions through various forms of advocacy directed at policymakers on behalf of another person, organization, or group.

Definition of Participants

These are the major actors and activities involved in lobbying. *Clients* (including individual persons or organized interests such as business corporations, trade associations, labor unions, and not-for-profit advocacy groups) retain *lobbyists* (including those employed in the government relations section of the client organization as well as outside individuals or firms). The lobbyist then develops various methods, strategies, and tactics (e.g., through design of a lobbying campaign) to

- gain access,
- inform,
- influence, and
- pressure.

These tactics are directed at *policymakers* (e.g., legislators or executive branch administrators and their staffs) who make policy decisions that affect the well-being of

- the client;
- the American public;
- the local, national, and international communities; and
- present and future generations of citizens.

Definition of Means and Ends

In the conduct of lobbying, the lobbyist uses various means, such as

- personal reputation,
- professional obligation,

- cultivated rapport, and
- financial inducement.

These assets are used to achieve selected political goals, such as the gaining of trust, which in turn can lead to "earned" access, through which the lobbyist can share information and opinions that influence the formation of public policy, or "positional" influence, which is based on one's standing in the public realm rather than earned through other means.

ORGANIZATION OF THE PRINCIPLES

The principles are divided into seven sections dealing with the following aspects of lobbying:

1. Lobbying and the common good
2. Lobbyist–client relationships
3. Lobbyist–policymaker relationships
4. Lobbyists and shapers of public opinion
5. Conflicts of interest
6. Lobbying strategies and tactics
7. The integrity of the lobbying profession

THE COMMON GOOD

As the preamble to the U.S. Constitution makes clear, the U.S. government is not a collective instrument for individual or group benefit but a carefully balanced network of free institutions deliberately designed to secure the common good. The common good—the comprehensive and enduring well-being of the political community as a whole—is the proper goal of public deliberation and action. It comprises a broad range of human "goods" to which the people are jointly committed and for which they accept final responsibility. The founders articulate these goods in memorable terms: "to form a more perfect Union, establish justice, insure domestic tranquility, provide for the common defense, promote the general welfare, and secure the blessings of liberty to ourselves and our posterity."

In a democratic society, it is in and through the shared deliberative activity of the people and their representatives that the common good is discovered and enacted. Public policy formation is a fallible but self-correcting process whereby ordinary citizens and their elected representatives seek to rise above private interests and desires to discern what is good for the country as a whole. This enlarged, public-spirited mentality is the hallmark of genuine political thinking. It is an essential part of civic virtue and a basic requirement for a sustainable democratic society.

THE PRINCIPLES

1. The pursuit of lobbying must take into account the common good, not merely a particular client's interests narrowly considered. A genuine commitment to the common good—the comprehensive and enduring well-being of the political community as a whole—by clients, lobbyists, and policymakers, is essential if the integrity of American democracy is to be preserved and enhanced. To secure this end, the concerns of all citizens who may be affected by specific legislative and policy decisions should be effectively represented in the decision-making process. In addition, our manner of financing political campaigns should not compromise elected officials or undermine public trust in their independence and impartiality.

   a. Because the purpose of lobbying is to influence the making of public policy, lobbyists should recognize that their responsibilities are different from those of an advocate in a purely private controversy between two adversaries, such as the parties to a lawsuit. By its nature, the lobbying process is designed to influence policymakers whose decisions and choices will have much broader political consequences.

   b. Therefore, in deciding whether to undertake an engagement or assignment and in determining what arguments to advance in support of, or in opposition to, a position, lobbyists should weigh the implications of their efforts for the well-being of the country as a whole; and they should inform both their client and the policymaker of the probable economic, social, and political consequences of the policy objectives being pursued

   c. The lobbyist should give special attention to the effects of government action or inaction on the least advantaged and most vulnerable citizens.

   d. While serving as an advocate for a client's position, the lobbyist retains a personal responsibility as a citizen for the fairness, integrity, and effectiveness of the policymaking process, as well as for the substantive political outcomes to which it leads.

2. The lobbyist-client relationship must be based on candor and mutual respect. The lobbyist should only undertake or pursue an assignment for a client whose senior management is genuinely committed to acceptable ethical conduct. The lobbyist has a responsibility to advise the client about the potentially harmful effects of the lobbying objectives, strategies, and tactics being considered. This principle applies not only to the client's explicit interests and public reputation, but also to the probable effect of the lobbying goals and strategies on the common good and on the legitimate concerns of other groups, especially the poor or underrepresented.

a. In determining whether to retain a particular lobbyist, a client should examine and evaluate the lobbyist's ethical history in the practice of lobbying. A client should not knowingly retain a lobbyist or lobbying firm found to have acted unethically without first candidly discussing this history with the lobbyist and evaluating the response.

b. In discussing potential retention by a prospective client, the lobbyist should not misrepresent the lobbyist's experience, political skills, and probable access in lobbying for a particular policy. If the lobbyist or the lobbyist's firm lacks adequate resources or the relevant political contacts to represent a client effectively on a particular matter, the lobbyist should inform the client or prospective client. The lobbyist should also inform the client or potential client of all prior lobbying efforts on the issue in which the lobbyist has engaged.

c. Before accepting an engagement or assignment from a prospective client, the lobbyist should examine and evaluate the prospective client's ethical history as it relates to lobbying. The lobbyist should not knowingly accept an engagement from a client found to have acted unethically, without first candidly discussing this history with the prospective client and evaluating the response.

d. The lobbyist should only undertake an assignment or continue with an assignment from a client to the extent that the lobbyist is satisfied that the senior management of the client is committed to acceptable ethical standards.

e. The lobbyist should inform the client about ethically acceptable lobbying options and strategies and give the client the opportunity, whenever appropriate, to choose between those options and strategies.

f. In formulating advice, the lobbyist is not limited only to issues of political feasibility and legal compliance but should also discuss the moral, economic, social, and civic factors that may be relevant to the client's situation and objectives.

g. The lobbyist should inform the client whether the proposed lobbying objectives and strategies are, in the lobbyist's judgment, ethically questionable.

h. The lobbyist has a responsibility to give advice to the client concerning the potentially harmful effects of the lobbying objectives, strategies, and tactics. This principle applies not only to the client's objectives and public reputation but also to the probable effects of the lobbying objectives and strategies on the common good or on the legitimate interests of other persons or groups, especially the poor or underrepresented.

i. The lobbyist should maintain appropriate confidentiality of client information and should not disclose confidential information without the client's informed consent.

j. The lobbyist should inform the client of all significant actions taken on its behalf, including coalitions formed and political contacts pursued.

k. It is wrong for the lobbyist to claim credit for accomplishments to which he or she did not contribute or to which the contribution was minimal.

3. A policymaker is entitled to expect candid disclosure from the lobbyist, including accurate and reliable information about the identity of the client and the nature and implications of the issues. Ethically responsible lobbying should serve a valuable educational function, because honest, well-informed lobbyists provide policymakers and their staffs with relevant information and incisive arguments and analysis bearing on matters of public debate.

a. In any presentations to a policymaker, the lobbyist should seek to provide factually correct, current, and accurate information. The lobbyist should not intentionally mislead or misinform any other party. It is wrong for the lobbyist to omit or fail to disclose information that is necessary to keep important statements made to the policymaker from being misleading.

b. To discharge these responsibilities, the lobbyist should undertake whatever inquiry is reasonably necessary to learn the salient facts bearing on the position being advanced and the statements being made.

c. The lobbyist should provide accurate and updated information to the policymaker if a change in the facts underlying important information that the lobbyist has already provided makes the information inaccurate, or if the lobbyist learns that the underlying facts were not as previously understood and that the information was inaccurate and the lobbyist knows that the policymaker may still be relying upon the information.

d. If the lobbyist believes that there is a substantial risk that the policymaker may be unaware of important information adverse to the position being advocated and that no one else is likely to bring that information to the policymaker's attention, the lobbyist should do so, but he or she may explain why the policymaker should not find the adverse information influential or decisive.

e. The lobbyist should not conceal or misrepresent the identity of the client whose interests and positions are being advanced. Because the policymaker's choice may turn not only on the arguments advanced by proponents and advocates of a position but also on their identity, the lobbyist should not participate in creating or representing a "front organization" that conceals the true identity of the clients whose interests and positions are being advanced.

f. The lobbying strategies used with policymakers should not compromise their real or perceived independence. This could occur in several ways, such as when fund-raising efforts or campaign contributions or the threat of negative publicity are linked to support for a particular policy objective.

4. In dealing with other shapers of public opinion, the lobbyist may not conceal or misrepresent the identity of the client or other pertinent facts. American public opinion is heavily influenced by the communications media. The democratic process requires that the policymaker, the communications media, and the American public be accurately informed about who is promoting a particular policy and who is funding and supporting the efforts made on its behalf. The use of the media in lobbying campaigns is therefore subject to the following:

a. The lobbyist may implement a strategy that involves attempting to influence policymakers though media reporting and editorial commentary. In pursuing such a strategy, the lobbyist should not engage in conduct with the media that would be improper if addressed directly to the policymaker. This principle includes the obligations to avoid misleading statements of fact and to avoid misrepresenting the identity of the client.

b. In dealing with the media on behalf of a client, and subject to the obligation to maintain the confidentiality of the client's confidential information, it is wrong for the lobbyist to intentionally obstruct or manipulate a journalist's efforts to seek accurate information that affects public policy decisions and to report on that information fairly and objectively.

c. It is wrong for the lobbyist to use campaign strategies that create unfair advantages in the decision-making process for their clients. Such strategies could include "phantom" grassroots campaigns, "front" groups intended to conceal the true identity of the clients whose interests are being advocated, saturation advertising that distorts the merits of a particular issue, unscrupulous pressure on public officials, and the inordinate expenditure of money to create a very uneven playing field. This principle is particularly important in the use of political advertising, because the public has the right to know the true identity of the clients whose interests are being advocated.

d. In the pursuit of the client's objectives, the lobbyist should show the same respect for the public and its right to accurate and relevant information as is shown to policymakers and their staffs.

5. *The lobbyist must avoid conflicts of interest.* In addition to civic obligations to country, the lobbyist has professional obligations to clients and personal obligations to his or her conscience. Fulfilling these diverse obligations may lead to conflicts of interest and responsibility.

a. Except with the informed consent of all of the clients or potential clients involved, it is wrong for the lobbyist to undertake or continue a representation that creates or is likely to create a conflict of interest.

b. A conflict of interest exists if the lobbyist will be called upon to advocate a position on an issue when the lobbyist is also representing another client on the same issue with a conflicting position or if the lobbyist's own personal beliefs, relationships, or interests—including a sense of civic obligation—are likely to compromise the effort with which the lobbyist advocates the client's position on an issue.

6. *Certain tactics are inappropriate in pursuing a lobbying engagement.* The responsible exercise of the lobbyist's First Amendment rights constrains the selection of lobbying strategies and tactics.

a. It is wrong knowingly to sponsor or disseminate false information about a candidate, person, or issue. Unless the information is not likely to be harmful to another person or to affect a policymaker's decision, the lobbyist must promptly take steps to rectify the situation after learning that he or she has disseminated such false information without knowing that it was false.

b. It is wrong to engage in attacks on a person's character, or participate in the process of doing so, unless the information offered is directly relevant to the merits of the issue being advocated.

c. It is wrong for the lobbyist to design a campaign that is intended to divert attention from the actual effects of the policy being advocated by focusing on irrelevant or "phantom" issues intended to frighten an interested party or to divert the public's attention from the true issues at stake.

d. Because a policymaker's judgment may appropriately consider not only the nature of a proposal but also the identity of the active proponents or opponents of a position, the integrity of the lobbying process requires that, except in extraordinary circumstances, the lobbyist should clearly identify all of the interests being represented in the attempt to influence policy.

7. The lobbyist has an obligation to promote the integrity of the lobbying profession and public understanding of the lobbying process. The lobbyist has an important and legitimate role to play in the American political process. At this time, public ignorance about and distrust of the lobbying profession are widespread. Many Americans are openly critical of lobbyists' political influence. Many other critics misunderstand the nature of the lobbying process and its appropriate role in shaping public policy. It is in the common interest of the lobbying profession and the American people that the public become better educated about the systemic effects of lobbying on the health of American democracy. The responsibility for this educational mission clearly rests in part with lobbyists themselves.

a. The lobbyist should help educate the public about the appropriate role of lobbying in a democratic society and should promote public understanding of and confidence in the lobbying process.

b. The lobbyist should be actively concerned not only to personally observe standards of ethical conduct but also to enhance the public image and reputation of the lobbying profession.

c. As a particularly active and influential participant in the democratic political process, the lobbyist should recognize that the quality, depth, and fairness of public debate on a question of public policy are more important than the quantity of pressure used to influence policymakers.

d. As a citizen engaged in a profession with a central role in the political process, the lobbyist should inform and educate both the client and the policymaker rather than simply reinforcing that person's preexisting views. The lobbyist should inform clients and public officials about any significant, unjust consequences of a policy position being advocated.

e. In dealing with other lobbyists, including those representing clients with adverse interests, the lobbyist should treat the other lobbyist as a professional colleague entitled to respect, refrain from misleading the other lobbyist, and avoid casting unwarranted aspersions on the integrity of the other lobbyist.

f. To promote the integrity of the profession, the lobbyist who obtains information establishing that another lobbyist has engaged in unlawful conduct as part of the lobbying process—including violation of the laws regarding bribery, gratuities, and reporting and disclosure—should bring this information to the attention of appropriate public officials charged with dealing with such violations.

NOTE

1. We owe some of this terminology to the work of William T. Murphy, Jr., derived from our interview with him on May 14, 1999, when he was director of the Lobbying Institute of the Center for Congressional and Presidential Studies at American University's School of Public Affairs in Washington.

8 CONCLUSION: DEMOCRATIC JUSTICE

> Now laws are said to be just both from the end (when, namely, they are ordained to the common good), from their author (. . . when the law does not exceed the power of the law-giver), and from their form (when, namely, burdens are laid on the subjects according to an equality of proportion).
>
> —Thomas Aquinas, *Summa Theologica*,
> first part of the second part, question 96, article 4

Why did we undertake this inquiry into the ethics of lobbying, and what did we learn from it? At the beginning, we were acutely aware of the growing importance of lobbying, of deliberate political advocacy, as a fact in American politics. Our original goal was to understand that fact in its many complex dimensions, to reach a fair and balanced appraisal of the lobbying process, and to recommend remedial measures for the conduct of lobbying if they were judged to be necessary.

Our inquiry was governed by two regulative principles. First, we cannot fairly appraise a complex human reality until we understand it, both from the inside, from the perspective of active participants, and from the outside, from the perspective of fair-minded observers. Starting from the experience and reflection of lobbyists themselves, we later consulted the empirical findings of those who have studied the role of lobbying in American democracy. Second, we wanted to understand lobbying both as an indispensable part of the policymaking process, but also in its broader institutional and cultural effects on the health of American democracy. Therefore, an explicitly civic intention, a strong desire to promote the public good, motivated our efforts from start to finish.

For the purpose of understanding contemporary political advocacy, we asked and tried to answer four questions:

- What is lobbying?
- How does it actually work in American politics today?
- Why has it become so influential in shaping the conduct of the federal government?
- What ethical and political challenges does it create for engaged participants and ordinary citizens?

As we proceeded from understanding to appraisal, we explicitly recognized the important and legitimate role of political advocacy in a representative democracy. The political right to petition the government for redress of grievances is deeply enshrined in Anglo-American law and tradition. The same is true for the right of voluntary association, the deliberate formation of civic groups to achieve common ends and purposes. In a continental democracy like the United States, intermediary bodies are clearly needed to connect U.S. citizens with the federal government in Washington. These intermediary bodies should be sources of reciprocal communication, informing the government of the opinions, needs, and concerns of a large and diverse citizenry—providing public officials, in turn, with an opportunity to educate the people in the conduct of government and on the complexity of national and international affairs. Intermediary bodies seek to lessen the remoteness and impersonality of government and to ensure the accountability of public officials to the citizens they represent.

We also distinguished between explicit political rights and their responsible exercise. The right of free speech, for example, does not entitle us to slander our neighbors or to cry "fire" in a crowded theatre. In seeking to clarify the responsible exercise of the right of political advocacy, we appealed to both law and ethics. Law articulates the prescriptions and prohibitions that govern the practice of lobbying. Ethics seeks to discover the ultimate justification for political advocacy: the human goods it is intended to promote, the individual rights it is required to respect, the obligations that attend the exercise of political rights, and the probable sources and consequences of explicit abuse. Violations of existing laws and rules are the clearest examples of the abuse of advocacy. But ethical norms and principles reveal that one can play by the rules and still engage in systematic unfairness. Adhering to the rules of the game provides a first approximation to justice, yet the rules themselves can be unfair, favoring one group to the systematic disadvantage of another. Consider segregation laws, or laws permitting the creation of monopolies and trusts.

INSIDERS AND OUTSIDERS

How did we finally appraise the achievements and limitations of the practice of lobbying in the United States? From the outset, we were struck by a noticeable split in the evaluative judgments of insiders and outsiders. Most of those presently engaged in the lobbying process, particularly corporate clients, experienced lobbyists, and public officials and their staffs, thought the system worked reasonably well (though there were numerous misgivings about the role of money in American political life).

More critical judgments were expressed by public interest groups, nonprofits, and advocates for the poor and disadvantaged. They thought the system unduly favored those with wealth, power, and abundant political resources. Several critical scholars believe that the system works to segregate "players" (who move in and out of the revolving governmental door) from ordinary citizens, particularly the poor, the unskilled, and the badly educated. They also acknowledge that the popular image of lobbying and lobbyists is probably out of date. Existing law and media scrutiny have made direct and explicit quid pro quo arrangements infrequent. Lobbying today is highly sophisticated and multidimensional, relying on a complex array of persuasive devices, many of them borrowed from the field of public relations. Though defenders of the system charge their critics with uninformed hyperbole, with misunderstanding how the lobbying process actually works, critical citizens from across the political spectrum strive to articulate their underlying intuition that the rules of the political game are not fair, that they unduly favor the wealthy and well positioned.

In a field as diverse and open-ended as lobbying, it is difficult to make a comprehensive assessment of collective performance. We simply do not know how to assess the probity and conduct of actively engaged lobbyists, many of them unregistered. Rather than passing judgment on the lobbying profession as a whole, we chose to articulate the internal principles and norms that properly govern the lobbying process. We based the Woodstock Principles on the conduct of lobbying at its best and on the traditional ideals of representative democracy.

We acknowledge a major incompleteness in our effort. We did not make specific recommendations about the financing of federal elections. Our silence on this fundamental matter should not be misconstrued. We recognize how important and how problematic the political role of money has become, but we had developed no consensus among ourselves or with those we interviewed on how best to address this critical national issue.

LETTER AND SPIRIT OF THE LAW

Explicit rules tell us what we must and must not do. Principles and precepts articulate the reasons behind our conduct and attempt to guide, inspire, and direct behavior in the thicket of daily life. The complexity of practical living and the multiple considerations that bear on human choice require that rules be wisely interpreted and principles flexibly applied. The ancient distinction between the letter and the spirit of the law remains in force. The point of the distinction is that those who act in the spirit of the law not only satisfy its explicit requirements but deliberately seek to promote the purposes for which the law was created. In a culture that celebrates the pursuit of self-interest and individual and corporate success, the spirit of the law, which properly looks to the common good, directly conflicts with the operative tendency to shape and apply existing rules in a way that favors private and partisan interests. This traditional conflict which is inseparable from politics explains why civic virtue is so important in public life. Civic virtue disposes those who make and influence public decisions to think, speak, and act on behalf of the commonweal.

The civic virtues of courage, moderation, wisdom, and justice are the practical excellences we expect in good citizens. We undertook this cooperative study not only as scholars and practitioners, but also as citizens dedicated to the ongoing American experiment in democracy. We share the hope of our nation's founders that popular government can achieve liberty and justice for all citizens. We also believe, as did the classical republican theorists, that justice is the appropriate standard of excellence for political communities. To make this commitment to justice specific and forceful, it is essential to articulate its criteria of application. Under what conditions is a decision-making process just? When are the laws and policies that issue from collective decisions reasonable and fair?

In his *Treatise on Law*, Thomas Aquinas identifies three fundamental criteria of political justice: the *end* for the sake of which law and policy are created; the author of the legislative or policy decision; the rational *form* of public edicts or laws (do they distribute public benefits and burdens in a proportional manner?). As Aquinas explains these criteria, he makes clear that the proper end of public decisions is to promote and secure the common good; that the authority of the legislator derives from his or her demonstrated independence and impartiality, from his or her consistently representing the concerns of the community as a whole; and that the distribution of public benefits and burdens is governed by the principle of proportionality. From those to whom much is given, much will be expected.

JUSTICE IN THE UNITED STATES TODAY

What insights do these criteria elicit when we examine the question of democratic justice in the United States? The most glaring tension can be simply stated. The majority of those who petition the government for assistance or relief are seeking to advance the private interest of their group or association. In contrast, government officials are responsible, in principle, for the comprehensive and enduring well-being of the national community. There is a striking disparity between the values and motives of market capitalism, with its imperative of self-interest and its focus on the bottom line, and the values and imperatives of political justice.

This disparity requires that democratic governments, though deeply attentive to the economic health and prosperity of the nation, remain clearly independent of the most powerful economic interests. On matters of taxation, environmental regulation, energy policy, and the distribution of public expenditures, the government must act—and be seen to act—on behalf of the people as a whole.

What legitimates the exercise of democratic power? Public officials derive their legitimacy from free and fair elections, from continuous public scrutiny of their decisions and actions, and from their responsiveness and accountability to the convictions and concerns of civil society. They must also be faithful to the laws and Constitution of the country and to the political principles on which the nation is founded. These principles include the political equality of all citizens and the equitable and balanced distribution of public power.

The balance of power envisaged by the founders operates both within and outside of government. The three distinct branches of the federal government are designed to prevent the monopoly or abuse of governmental authority. The intermediary associations of civil society exercise public scrutiny over government and are subject, in turn, to political scrutiny as circumstances warrant. As we have noted, democratic justice requires that political power remain independent of the dominant economic interests. Governmental oversight and regulation are needed to check abuses of economic power and to ensure that free and fair markets as well as reasonable working conditions are consistently maintained.

Although the financing of public elections is outside of the scope of our study, one of the clear dangers posed by soft money and by politically influential corporate lobbying is that political and economic power will coalesce to the benefit of the privileged few and the disadvantage of the national majority.

Public confidence in democratic government rests on the belief that the needs and concerns of all citizens are accorded equal weight, that the requirements of political equality are actually met. The people also need to be convinced that economic and political power are fairly distributed, and that public officials remain effectively independent of the organized interests they are expected to regulate.

Social and economic justice require the fair distribution of the benefits and burdens of human cooperation. In a democracy, the regulative principle is that of civic equality, equality under the law, equality of opportunity, and the equal treatment of participants in the many sectors of institutional life. Democratic equality, however, is in practice complex. In some cases, where no distinction is made among citizens, the appropriate form of equality is arithmetic; for example, equality of individual rights and liberties and equality of political representation (one person–one vote). But in those domains where relevant distinctions exist among citizens, the appropriate form of equality is geometric or proportional. In the distribution of public benefits, such as honors, offices, and income, those who contribute more to the collective good are entitled to receive more in return. But the benefits they receive should be proportional to their contribution. The same principle applies to the sharing of public burdens such as taxation or pro bono service. Those citizens who are better able to bear the burden should carry the heavier load. Everyone should contribute in accordance with their ability and resources; no one should carry a disproportionate share, but from those to whom much is given much will be expected in return.

Political solidarity in a democracy rests on the achievement of economic and social justice. There needs to be a reasonably equitable distribution of wealth, income, opportunity, and economic security, with the guarantee of a decent minimum for all. Disproportionate inequality in the distribution of public goods and obligations is both politically and socially unwise. Politically, it severely erodes public trust in the legitimacy of both government and business; socially, it creates dangerous cycles of poverty, alienation, and crime. The radical and accelerating inequality of wealth and income in the United States, and the fear that economic inequality translates directly into substantive political inequality, raise legitimate and serious concerns about the justice and health of our democracy.

These justice-based concerns are relevant to all citizens: to clients, lobbyists, public officials, scholars and critics, and the nation as a whole. Preserving and strengthening the soundness of our democracy is a shared responsibility. Correcting failures in democratic justice will require individual, institutional, and cultural change. Individuals will need to think and act more like citizens than petitioners or consumers. Structural inequities in our political and economic institutions will need to be remedied in a democratic fashion (to paraphrase Madison, we are seeking democratic remedies for democratic ills), and the intrusion of the capitalist values of self-interest and unbridled competition into our civic culture will need to be resisted by a resurgence of civic virtues and a renewal of public spirit. The great challenges to the American democratic experiment vary from generation to generation. In our time, we are not called to end slavery, to overcome economic depression, or to resist the totalitarian menace. The challenge we face is to create economic justice and enduring political solidarity in an era of comparative peace and prosperity. Until we meet this democratic challenge, the historic American promise of liberty and justice for all will remain unfulfilled.

W O O D S T O C K

Theological Center

Publications in Ethics

The Ethics of Lobbying: Organized Interests, Political Power, and the Common Good
Georgetown University Press, 2002

Ethical Issues in Managed Health Care Organizations
Georgetown University Press, 1999

Ethical Considerations in the Business Aspects of Health Care
Georgetown University Press, 1995

Creating and Maintaining an Ethical Corporate Climate
Georgetown University Press, 1990

ORDER FORM

TITLE	COST	QTY.	PRICE	TOTAL
The Ethics of Lobbying: Organized Interests, Political Power, and the Common Good	$12.00/copy $10.00/copy, bulk orders of 20 or more			
Ethical Issues in Managed Health Care Organizations	$8.00/copy $6.00/copy, bulk orders of 20 or more			
Ethical Considerations in the Business Aspects of Health Care	$6.00/copy $3.00/copy, bulk orders of 20 or more			
Creating and Maintaining an Ethical Corporate Climate	$5.00/copy $3.00/copy, bulk orders of 20 or more			

Postage/handling ($4.00 single, + $1 each for bulk order)   Postage/handling_____

Total_____

Make check payable to **Woodstock Theological Center**, Box 571137, Georgetown University, Washington, DC 20057-1137

NAME: _____

ORGANIZATION: _____

ADDRESS/CITY/STATE/ZIP: _____

TELEPHONE: _____ E-MAIL: _____

Telephone 202-687-3532 · Fax 202-687-5835 · E-mail: wtc@gusun.georgetown.edu · http://www.georgetown.edu/centers/woodstock/